Public Choice – A Primer

Public Choice – A Primer

EAMONN BUTLER

The Institute of Economic Affairs

First published in Great Britain in 2012 by
The Institute of Economic Affairs
2 Lord North Street
Westminster
London SW1P 3LB
in association with Profile Books Ltd

The mission of the Institute of Economic Affairs is to improve public understanding of the fundamental institutions of a free society, with particular reference to the role of markets in solving economic and social problems.

A CIP catalogue record for this book is available from the British Library.

ISBN 978 0 255 36650 2
eISBN 978 0 255 36677 9

Many IEA publications are translated into languages other than English or are reprinted. Permission to translate or to reprint should be sought from the Director General at the address above.

Typeset in Stone by MacGuru Ltd
info@macguru.org.uk

Printed and bound in Britain by Hobbs the Printers

CONTENTS

About the IEA

THE AUTHOR

Eamonn Butler is director of the Adam Smith Institute, a leading policy think tank. He has degrees in economics, philosophy and psychology, gaining a PhD from the University of St Andrews in 1978. During the 1970s he worked for the US House of Representatives, and taught philosophy at Hillsdale College, Michigan, before returning to the UK to help found the Adam Smith Institute.

Eamonn is author of books on the pioneering economists Milton Friedman, F. A. Hayek and Ludwig von Mises, and a primer on the Austrian School of Economics. For the IEA, he has written primers on Adam Smith and Ludwig von Mises. He is co-author of a history of wage and price controls, and of a series of books on IQ. His recent popular publications, *The Best Book on the Market*, *The Rotten State of Britain* and *The Alternative Manifesto*, have attracted considerable attention, and he is a frequent contributor to print and broadcast media.

ACKNOWLEDGEMENTS

Thanks go to John Meadowcroft and Charles K. Rowley for their early advice and input, and to Madsen Pirie, Sally Thompson and Rachel Moran for their helpful comments on the draft text.

FOREWORD

Within the last week the British prime minister has made two major statements expressing the opinion that it is the job of government to identify and correct market failure. There are several important critiques of this approach to government. The Austrian critique argues that the market is a *process* of competition and, if perfect competition does not exist, we cannot know the outcome that would have arisen had it existed. Therefore the government cannot correct market failure; it can merely remove the barriers to the competitive process that it erects. Where market failure is perceived as arising from externalities, it can also be argued that you need a market to discover the value of those externalities to the people affected. Government cannot easily second-guess this value.

Perhaps the easiest critique to understand conceptually, however, comes from the Public Choice school. At one level, Public Choice economics simply asks us to make the same assumptions about human behaviour in the political sphere as we make when we analyse markets. For example, monopolies would not lead to the problems identified in the textbooks if self-interested owners did not try to maximise profits; carbon dioxide outputs would not worry us so much if consumers did not try to maximise their consumption for given income levels; bank failures would not worry us if banks did not respond to government guarantees by increasing the risks they take. In other words, if self-interest did not operate within the market, so-called market failure would not give rise to the sort of problems that our prime minister and others identify – though it may give rise to other problems.

But if self-interest gives rise to certain outcomes in markets which some believe cause problems that politicians should try to fix, should we not assume that these same forces of self-interest exist within the political systems that try to 'correct' market failure? As soon as this is appreciated, surely it is a 'game changer' in the debate about the appropriateness of government intervention – we can no longer assume that a beneficent and omniscient government can improve upon the market outcome. Government decisions will themselves be affected by the self-interest of politicians, voters, bureaucrats, regulators and so on. When did you ever see voters in one constituency demonstrating to support the closure of their hospital so that health services in other constituencies can be improved?

This self-interest operating in the political system will lead to 'government failure', which can be far more serious than 'market failure' because of the coercive power that government exercises and because government is not subject to a direct competitive process. It is possible, in a representative democracy, for the self-interest of a very small number to lead to decisions being taken that could be to the detriment of the majority. It could certainly be argued, for example, that Scottish members of the UK parliament and members of parliament around Heathrow airport have exercised enormous power in recent years because of their pivotal role in determining how a parliamentary majority is put together.

Public Choice economics has come a long way since my predecessor, Arthur Seldon, introduced what was then called 'the Economics of Politics' to the UK. There are many university departments that specialise in this subject area as well as learned journals. While those ground-breaking publications by Tullock, Buchanan and others were very important in changing the climate of opinion (influencing, for example, the creators of the television series *Yes, Minister* and *Yes, Prime Minister*), it is now important for the IEA to publish an up-to-date summary of the discipline which is accessible to a wide audience.

Eamonn Butler's excellent primer is ideal for students, teachers and opinion formers. It is also useful for those politicians and regulators who have the humility to wish to explore the limits of government action. This primer explores the potential implications for government policy of the application of self-interest within the political system; it discusses how political systems could be designed so that they bring about the right balance of government action and restraint; and it examines how government decision-making can be constrained to those areas where collective action is desirable.

It is vital that these issues are better understood in order that we have more humility in government and political systems that are better designed. The arguments are relevant, for example, to the debate over Scottish devolution as well as to the debate surrounding tax transfers to Scotland in the current settlement. They are also highly relevant to debates over the governance of the European Union. It is to be hoped that this primer will promote a wider understanding of the nature of the processes that take place within government and that this, in turn, makes it less likely that we will have governments that see market failure everywhere and lack any sense of proportion about the ability of government to correct it.

Eamonn Butler's primer on Public Choice is an excellent contribution to explaining this increasingly complex subject to a wider audience, which the IEA is delighted to publish.

PHILIP BOOTH

Editorial and Programme Director,
Institute of Economic Affairs
Professor of Insurance and Risk Management,
Cass Business School
January 2012

The views expressed in this monograph are, as in all IEA publications, those of the authors and not those of the Institute (which has no corporate view), its managing trustees, Academic Advisory Council Members or senior staff.

SUMMARY

- Public Choice applies the *methods* of economics to the *theory and practice* of politics and government. This approach has given us important insights into the nature of democratic decision-making.
- Just as self-interest motivates people's private commercial choices, it also affects their communal decisions. People also 'economise' as voters, lobby groups, politicians and officials, aiming to maximise the outcome they personally desire, for minimum effort. Consequently the well-developed tools of economics – such as profit and loss, price and efficiency – can be used to analyse politics too.
- Collective decision-making is necessary in some areas. However, the fact that the market may fail to provide adequately in such areas does not necessarily mean that government can do things better. There is 'government failure' too. Political decision-making is not a dispassionate pursuit of the 'public interest', but can involve a struggle between different personal and group interests.
- There is no single 'public interest' anyway. We live in a world of value-pluralism: different people have different values and different interests. Competition between competing interests is inevitable. This makes it vital to study how such competing interests and demands are resolved by the political process.

- The self-interest of political parties lies in getting the votes they need to win power and position. They may pursue the 'median voter' – the position at the centre, where voters bunch. Government officials will also have their own interests, which may include maximising their budgets.
- In this struggle between interests, small groups with sharply focused interests have more influence in decision-making than much larger groups with more diffused concerns, such as consumers and taxpayers. The influence of interest groups may be further increased because electors are 'rationally ignorant' of the political debate, knowing that their single vote is unlikely to make a difference, and that the future effects of any policy are unpredictable.
- Because of the enormous benefits that can be won from the political process, it is rational for interest groups to spend large sums on lobbying for special privileges – an activity known as 'rent seeking'.
- Interest groups can increase their effect still further by 'logrolling' – agreeing to trade votes and support each other's favoured initiatives. These factors make interest group minorities particularly powerful in systems of representative democracy, such as legislatures.
- In direct democracy, using mechanisms such as referenda, the majority voting rule that is commonly adopted allows just 51 per cent of the population to exploit the other 49 per cent – as in the old joke that 'democracy is two wolves and a sheep deciding who shall eat whom for dinner'. In representative democracies, much smaller proportions of the electorate can have undue influence.
- Because of the problem of minorities being exploited – or

[handwritten margin note: Small groups]

minorities exploiting majorities – many Public Choice theorists argue that political decision-making needs to be constrained by constitutional rules.

Public Choice – A Primer

1 WHAT IS PUBLIC CHOICE?

Public Choice is often referred to as a school of economics. In fact, it is more an approach to political science. It does not try to explain how the economy works. Rather, Public Choice uses the *methods* and *tools* of economics to explore how *politics and government* works. It is an approach that produces some surprising insights, and throws up challenging questions – such as how efficient, effective and indeed legitimate the political process really is.

Why use economics?

It may seem odd to use economics to analyse politics and government. To most people, economics is all about money, the market and business economy, and private gain. Government is supposed to be about benefiting the whole public, in non-financial ways, and through non-profit means.

But economics is not just about money. The word itself comes from the Greek *oikonomia*, meaning the management of a household – where the aim is family contentment, rather than financial profit, and where many different factors, human as well as financial, have to be balanced.

Every day, we make similar choices. Will the view from the next hill be worth the effort of climbing it? How much time should we spend in finding exactly the right birthday card for a friend?

No money is at stake, yet these are still *economic* decisions in the broad sense of the word. They involve us weighing up how much time or effort we think it worth spending to achieve our aims, and choosing between the different possibilities. Economics is actually about how we choose to spend any available resources (such as our time or effort) in trying to achieve other things that we value more highly – it is not just about financial choices.

Economists have developed some simple but very useful tools for this task. They include such concepts as *opportunity cost* – the value you place on whatever you have to sacrifice (e.g. time or effort) in order to achieve some end; and *benefit* – the value of what you gain (e.g. the right birthday card or a fine view). Likewise, the difference between the value you set on what you give up and on what you gain is your *profit* – though if you could not find a nice card, or the view disappointed, it could equally be your *loss*. And economists say that when people make choices, they consciously seek to exchange things they value less for things they value more: in other words, they are *rational* and *self-interested*.

Applying economics to politics

Public Choice is about applying these simple economic concepts to the study of how *collective* choices are made – applying them to such things as the design and workings of constitutions, election mechanisms, political parties, interest groups, lobbying, bureaucracy, parliaments, committees and other parts of the governmental system. Collective, *political* decisions, such as whether to raise property taxes to build a new road, are just as *economic* as any other: they too involve a choice between *costs* and *benefits*, not just financial costs and benefits, but, more broadly, between whatever has to be sacrificed and whatever is gained as a result.

Yet there is a twist. When someone makes an economic choice, they personally experience both the costs (e.g. time or effort) and the benefits (e.g. the view or the right card).[1] In public choices, by contrast, the people who benefit (e.g. the road's users) are not always the people who bear the cost (e.g. homeowners). Also, in the market both sides in a transaction have to agree to it – if either the buyer or the seller is less than content, they can simply walk away from the deal. In politics, by contrast, the minority cannot walk away: they are forced to accept the decision of the majority, and bear whatever sacrifices that collective choice demands.

Sadly, that makes it perfectly possible for a self-interested majority to exploit the minority, by voting themselves public benefits that impose financial or other burdens on other people. Road users might want a new highway, for example, which will cut through the gardens, or raise the taxes, of other people who might never use it or benefit from it. What makes it so important to study how such government decisions are made is the fact that government can use coercion to force minorities to go along with the majority decision. It gives power to majorities which might well be wielded responsibly – but which they could also use to vote themselves benefits and pass the costs on to others.

By using economic theory to explore how government decisions are made, Public Choice theory can help us to understand this process, to identify problems such as the self-interest of particular groups and the potential exploitation of coerced minorities, and

1   There are, of course, 'external' or 'social' costs and benefits of such economic actions. But these tend to be a small aspect of the total costs and benefits of most transactions. Where they are large, the government often seeks to intervene. However, as will immediately become clear, an important theme of Public Choice economics is that such government action also has external costs and benefits.

to propose ways of limiting these shortcomings. In recognition of this important role, the American economist James M. Buchanan received the 1986 Nobel Prize in Economic Sciences for his work in explaining the nature of exploitation in electoral systems, the self-interest of politicians and bureaucrats, the power of interest groups, and the potential role that constitutional restraints could have in limiting their malign effect on public decision-making.

The Public Choice challenge to orthodox thinking

Post-war 'welfare' economists strove hard to measure the costs and benefits of policy proposals such as new roads or airports, and to identify how 'social welfare' – the well-being of the community as a whole – might be increased and maximised by the right choices. This work, they believed, would inform and improve public decision-making.

A key and unspoken assumption of this approach, however, was that such policy decisions would be made logically and rationally, by enlightened and impartial officials, pursuing the public interest. That in turn would make them far superior to market choices, driven as they were by self-interest and private profit.

Public Choice shattered this assumption. It accepted that collective decisions are needed for some tasks that inevitably require communal action. But it showed how the process of making those decisions falls far short of the welfare economists' assumed ideal. As Public Choice scholars pointed out, the people who make public decisions are, in fact, just as self-interested as anyone else. They are, after all, the same people; individuals do not suddenly become angels when they get a job in government. Public Choice does not necessarily argue that all actions to influence government policy are self-interested, merely that we should not assume that people behave differently in the marketplace for goods and services from how they behave when influencing government decisions. It is prudent to assume that self-interest might motivate people.] *Self interest*

Of course, being *self-interested* does not imply that people are *selfish*. They may care very deeply about other people and may well want to help their friends, family and community, rather than just benefit themselves. But the point is that *whatever* it is that they want to achieve – from personal wealth to community harmony – it is sensible to assume that they will try to act deliberately and effectively in ways that will increase it. As economists put it, they are *rational maximisers*.

It shocked orthodox thinkers when Buchanan, with his co-author Gordon Tullock, applied this 'economic' view of human beings systematically through the institutions of government – suggesting that legislators, officials and voters all use the political process to advance their private interests, just as they do in the marketplace. Even more shocking was their conclusion that political decisions, far from being made efficiently and dispassionately in pursuit of the 'public interest', could well be less efficient, less rational and more vulnerable to manipulation by vested interests than the supposedly flawed market process.] *Public interest*

Public or private interests?

Public Choice, then, looks at how the motivations of individuals affect the outcome of their collective decision-making. It rejects the idea that politics is a process by which we somehow discover what is truly in the 'public interest'.

For a start, what can 'public interest' possibly mean? If one large group of people wants a new road, but another is violently opposed and wants lower taxes instead, while a third thinks the money should be spent on defence, a fourth on hospitals and a fifth wishes the money to be split between welfare and education, it is plainly impossible to translate those clashing opinions into any sensible policy that represents the 'public interest'. We live in a world of value-pluralism and, as far as economic decisions taken by government are concerned, people value different goods and services differently. Inevitably, the different interests of different people will clash and agreement on what constitutes the 'public interest' is impossible.

It is the 'sheep and two wolves' problem. As the old joke goes, democracy is like a sheep and two wolves deciding who will eat whom for dinner. Their utterly contradictory views cannot be netted off into some measure of the 'social welfare' of the 'sheep and wolf community'. Public Choice scholars maintain that welfare economists got into a muddle because they forgot that only *individuals* have motivations – not groups. *Individuals* have interests and beliefs and values; a *group* has no interests or beliefs or values of its own – only those of the individuals who comprise it. Likewise, only *individuals* choose – when they vote at elections, for example. *Groups* as such do not choose; a *group* does not go into the polling booth.

According to Public Choice, then, voting and legislating are processes in which *individuals* can pursue their own, often conflicting, interests. There is no objective communal 'public interest' hovering around, which voting somehow discovers. Indeed, different decision-making systems will produce very different policy choices.

For example, under direct democracy using simple majority voting – say, a referendum on whether a new road should be built – the majority can dominate the minority. If 51 per cent of the voters vote for building a new road, that is what will be done, even if the other 49 per cent disapprove, and no matter how strongly they disapprove. If, instead, the decision has to be unanimous, then any one objector can veto the proposal. And with a two-thirds majority rule, the pro-road lobby might have to modify their proposals in order to reach a compromise with the objectors. In other words, each system produces a different outcome: one cannot hail any of them as discovering *the* objective and incontrovertible 'public interest'. Each system just reflects the multiplicity of people's preferences in different ways.

Accordingly, Public Choice does not itself aim to deliver some will-o'-the-wisp 'social welfare' or 'public interest'. It seeks only to inform the political debate by explaining the different dynamics between motivated individuals that emerge under different political institutions, and by outlining the different outcomes that arise as a result.

The calculus of voting

One early conclusion of this analysis is that, even at the best of times, voting may not reflect the true views of the electorate. As Public Choice scholars point out, people often vote tactically in elections, rather than in line with their true opinions. For example, they may calculate that their preferred option or candidate has little chance of winning, and vote for one they deeply dislike in order to keep out another that they really hate.

Another conclusion is that voters in small groups who share

very strong private interests may have a voting power that far exceeds their number. People who would benefit from a new road, for example, have a powerful, direct incentive to raise funds and campaign strongly for the project. By contrast, the great mass of taxpayers may figure that the cost of the project will be spread thinly between them all; so, even though they are by far the majority, they will have much less incentive to campaign against the project, or even turn out to vote, and their dissent will go largely unstated and unheard.

Interest groups may also form alliances to create majority coalitions. Different groups who each want new roads in their area, say, may get together to form a broad pro-road campaign that, if successful, will benefit them all. Candidates for office too may try to create an electoral majority by bidding for the support of different groups with strong, motivating interests. This gives minorities a particularly powerful influence in systems of representative democracy, such as elections of candidates to a legislature. While majorities dominate direct democracy, minorities dominate representative democracy.

Going for votes

Public Choice also tells us something about the motivations of political parties, politicians and officials. Political parties, for example, have a very strong objective of their own – to get elected. Their best chance of that, suggest Public Choice theorists, may be to adopt policies that appeal to the large mass of voters in the centre, which also leaves them some hope of picking up voters on either side. But this pursuit of the 'median voter' means that parties tend to bunch at the centre at elections, leaving non-centrist electors largely unrepresented.

And once elected, politicians may well resort to vote-trading (or 'logrolling') to get their own policies through the legislature. They agree to support measures that other legislators strongly favour in return for those legislators' support on their own preferred projects. The simple deal is 'you vote for my measures and I'll vote for yours', but the result is that more legislation is passed than anyone really wants.

The growth of government is also promoted by the self-interest of civil servants. They seek the security and status of a large department with a big budget, say many Public Choice scholars, which is why they so often talk legislators into expanding the regulations and laws that they administer. Again, what is missing in this process is the voice of the public who have to pay for these measures and who suffer their effects.] Civil Servants

The power of Public Choice

Public Choice economics is having a powerful impact on political science. It has led to some major rethinking of the very nature of elections, legislatures and bureaucracies; and on whether the political process can claim to be in any way superior to the market process. And the issues it raises, especially the prospect of minorities being exploited by coalitions of interest groups, lead some Public Choice theorists to advocate strong constitutional restraints on government and the political process.

2 PUBLIC CHOICE – THE BIOGRAPHY

Intellectuals have long placed great faith in government. From Plato's vision of 'philosopher kings' onwards, their main concern was merely how to get the right people into office – and to focus them on doing the right things. In early modern times, social thinkers took it for granted that public servants would be objective and fair, so focused mainly on their *moral* responsibilities. Niccolò Machiavelli's 1532 book *The Prince* was an exception; but that was widely dismissed as a scandalous travesty of real government.

Gradually, however, more thinkers began to question the probity of the political system itself, and the vested interests of those it put into power. In his 1742 essay on parliament, the Scottish philosopher David Hume denounced the self-interest of people in government positions, and urged that, for our own protection, we should treat them as if they were 'knaves'. And in his 1776 *The Wealth of Nations*, Adam Smith strongly criticised the cosy relationship between business and government, in which those in authority would grant monopolies to favoured courtiers and manufacturers.

Precursors of modern Public Choice

The questions raised by Hume and Smith about the workings of the political process remain central to Public Choice theory today; but the more direct origin of modern Public Choice can be traced back to the thoughts of two eighteenth-century French mathematicians on the mechanics of voting and elections.

In 1785, the Marquis de Condorcet noted the problem of *cycling*. To illustrate this idea, suppose that a community uses majority rule to decide between three policy options or election candidates: let us call them Rock, Paper and Scissors. As in the modern game, it is perfectly possible that Rock would lose to Paper in a vote between the two, Paper would lose to Scissors, and yet Scissors would lose to Rock. Which, then, would be the legitimate winner? There is no clear choice that trumps all others. As different pairs were put up for vote, we would *cycle* from one winner, to the next, to the next.

In 1781, Jean-Charles de Borda had also speculated about the nature of elections – in particular, the problem that even if some voters feel very strongly about an issue, they still get only one vote, just like those who are largely unconcerned. He proposed instead a system in which people rank the options or candidates, and their votes would then be weighted accordingly. In a three-way election, for example, candidates would get two points for every first preference, one point for every second preference, and zero points for every third preference; the winner would be the one that accumulated most points.

A century passed before the Oxford mathematician Charles Dodgson (more widely known as the *Alice in Wonderland* author Lewis Carroll) rediscovered these French texts. He wrote several items on voting procedures and, in 1876, proposed a complex system to overcome Condorcet's *cycling* paradox.

Another key text was an 1896 essay on the just distribution

of tax by the Swedish economist Knut Wicksell. Though largely a work of economics, it raised the Public Choice problem that a majority in power could, if they wished, unfairly shift the burden of taxation on to the minority. Wicksell concluded that only *unanimous* agreement could prevent minorities being exploited. It is an idea that still underpins much Public Choice thinking today.

Modern Public Choice thinkers

A further half-century would go by, however, before the Scottish economist Duncan Black rediscovered Borda's and Condorcet's ideas again, and made them widely available to the English-speaking world. Black's 1948 articles on the electoral problems that Borda and Condorcet posed make him arguably the founder of modern Public Choice.

Black's most important contribution to Public Choice theory is his famous *median voter theorem*. This suggests that on straightforward issues – such as how much should be spent on roads – the political parties will gravitate to the centre of opinion, where most votes are to be had. Any party that drifts away from the centre will lose votes to the other side. And since political parties aim to win votes, the result is that parties bunch together at the centre, giving voters little real choice.

In 1951, the American economist (and later Nobel laureate) Kenneth Arrow made another major contribution with his *impossibility theorem*. The key question for any electoral system is how accurately the group decisions that emerge from it reflect the nature, prevalence and strength of preferences among the members of the voting public.

Arrow showed that there really is no practical democratic

system that can guarantee this happy outcome. Some later theorists have shared this gloomy conclusion, arguing, for example, that *any* election system can be manipulated by people voting strategically, or by *agenda-setters* who decide the order in which decisions are taken (a particular problem in committees).

One of Arrow's students, Anthony Downs, also worked on the median-voter issue, but is best known for his 1957 application of *rational choice theory* across the workings of the political marketplace. *Rational choice* means action that is deliberately and efficiently tailored to achieving a person's objectives. For political parties, thought Downs, those objectives are the income, prestige and power they gain from being in office – rather than any particular policies. Indeed, they would change their policies in search of the votes that would put them in government. Voters, for their part, would rationally choose whichever party delivered them most benefits.

Downs's most famous idea, however, is that of the *rational ignorance* of voters. He pointed out that it takes time and effort for voters to find out what policies each candidate supports. But the chance of any one person's vote actually deciding an election is microscopic. It is simply not worth voters' time and effort to become well informed. As a result, many people vote on the basis of party labels, or do not vote at all. Sadly, this means that since most voters are apathetic, well-informed interest groups can exert a disproportionate influence on the parties.

Buchanan and Tullock

Their 1962 book *The Calculus of Consent* made the US authors James Buchanan and Gordon Tullock the leading figures in Public

Choice. In the book, they explored the issues raised by simple majority voting systems, and examined in depth the phenomenon of logrolling. But their main contribution was to separate the *constitutional* stage in which the voting rules are decided from the subsequent votes that are taken under those rules. They insisted that a constitution must require *unanimous* agreement: otherwise, the majority could design a system by which the minority could be exploited in future votes.

Buchanan and Tullock saw the political system and the evolution of constitutions as a process by which *individuals* seek to protect their own interests, rather than one in which we all strive to achieve some conception of the 'public interest'. Their approach challenged the prevailing view that widespread government intervention was needed to improve social welfare by correcting cases of 'market failure'. The real problem, they insisted, was *government failure*. Problems such as monopolies, externalities (the harmful side effects of other people's actions) and limited or one-sided information were much more evident in government than in markets. And because of the winner-takes-all nature of public decisions, the opportunity to escape from them was much less.

Schools and prizes

Between them, Buchanan and Tullock founded what is known as the 'Virginia School' of Public Choice, which focuses on constitutional theory and real-world political institutions. There is also the 'Rochester School', which applies statistics and mathematical techniques to the subject, and the 'Chicago School', which concentrates more on the pure economic theory of collective decision-making.

When Buchanan was awarded the 1986 Nobel Prize in Economic Sciences for his work on Public Choice, many people questioned why Tullock had not shared it. Whatever the reasons, Tullock's own contributions to Public Choice are very notable. For example, he made important original contributions on the issue of 'rent seeking' (see below) – the widespread but wasteful activity whereby interest groups use the political process to win themselves monopolies and privileges.

The power of interest groups

In a 1965 book, *The Logic of Collective Action*, the American economist Mancur Olson also explored the impact of special interest groups on the political process. The fact that lobby groups exist is obvious enough. But Olson showed that there are many large interest groups who find it hard to mount effective lobbying campaigns. These include important groups such as consumers and taxpayers.

One reason is the *free-rider* problem: if a consumer lobby were successful in winning concessions from politicians, *all* consumers would benefit, whether or not they actively joined the campaign. So, why should anyone make any contribution, when they can free-ride on the efforts of others? The disturbing result is that those groups, such as professional bodies and trade unions, that can somehow restrict any benefits they achieve to their own members, are over-represented in the public debate. But those, such as consumers and taxpayers, that are more numerous but harder to organise are under-represented.

In 1962 the American political scientist William H. Riker – the leading figure in the Rochester School – explored how interest groups might form coalitions, offering to support each other for mutual advantage in the political process. Alliances take effort to set up and keep together, however, and Riker found that 'grand coalitions' are short-lived. He concluded that the best strategy for interest groups was to assemble a *minimum winning coalition* – an alliance just large enough to win, but not too big to keep together.

Riker also brought *game theory* into Public Choice – the mathematical modelling of situations, as in elections, where an individual's decisions depend in part on the decisions made by others.

Bureaucracy and regulation

A further disturbing feature of government is that public officials also have their own interests. The American economist William A. Niskanen tried to identify the interests and objectives of bureaucrats in a 1971 book, *Bureaucracy and Representative Government*. He suggested that people in public agencies seek to maximise their budgets – which brings with it power, status, comfort, security and other benefits. They have the advantage over legislators in budget negotiations, he thought, because they know more about their agencies' functions than legislators do, as the latter are inevitably generalists. And once the politicians have committed to a policy, bureaucrats can crank up the implementation budget, knowing that the politicians will not want the public humiliation of abandoning the project. The result is a larger and less efficient bureaucracy than electors actually want.

A 1971 article, by George Stigler, marked the arrival of the Chicago School and criticised bureaucracy from another point of view. Building on the interest group theories of Mancur Olson, Stigler concluded that regulation would come to serve special interests, rather than the general public. The concentrated interests of professional groups, such as doctors or pharmaceutical companies, give them a strong incentive to organise and to lobby politicians, who, in turn, set up regulatory agencies to buy them off. It is not so much that agencies become captured by special interests; the problem is that agencies are set up from the start specifically to benefit those interests. Stigler summed this view up by saying in his article:[1] 'as a rule, regulation is acquired by industry, and is designed and operated primarily for its benefit'.

Recent reconsiderations

Such ideas left Public Choice scholars pessimistic about the public decision-making process. It seemed impossible to identify any system that would generate collective choices that truly and consistently reflected the range of individuals' preferences. People would vote strategically instead of showing their true preferences; interest groups would have undue influence; the mass of the public would have little incentive to understand the issues or even to vote; agenda-setters would ensure that their own preferences prevailed; parties would converge to the centre instead of offering a real choice; lobbyists would spend vast resources on seeking favours from politicians; and bureaucrats would feather their own nests.

Nevertheless, other Public Choice theorists have been more optimistic. Back in the 1940s, Joseph A. Schumpeter claimed that the competition for votes actually produces a rather beneficial outcome, like the 'invisible hand' of competition in the

---

1   The article was called 'The theory of economic regulation' and was published in the *Bell Journal of Economics and Management Science*, 2: 137–46.

marketplace. And more recently, some such as Peter Coughlin and Shmuel Nitzan have pointed out that when there is a large variety of issues that parties can stake out for their own, there is much less chance of 'cycling' deadlock. Others such as Edward H. Clarke and Theodore Groves have explored different ways in which voters might be induced to show their real preferences, and take account of the cost that their demands would impose on others, rather than vote selfishly and strategically.

Practical testing has added to the optimism. For example, some scholars now argue that bureaucrats and their budgets are in fact much better controlled than Niskanen feared. And, rather than buzzing constantly around the median voter, political parties actually do diverge, significantly and long-term, on important issues such as inflation and unemployment.

New approaches

The pioneers of modern Public Choice theory were all either British or American, and focused on the workings of two-party, simple majority systems. But Public Choice has grown international, and now looks much more to the multi-party systems and diverse voting rules that prevail in many other places. Among the key issues today, for example, are how multi-party coalitions are built, how stable they are, and why many parties choose to run minority governments, rather than enter into coalitions.

As well as the evidence from real political systems, economists such as Vernon Smith (winner of the 2002 Nobel Prize) have conducted practical experiments on how people – usually their students – actually make choices. Among the insights that have emerged is that it *is* possible to design election systems that reveal the strength of different electors' views and discourage strategic voting, and that Buchanan and Tullock's ideal of unanimous agreement on a constitution is in fact feasible. And many other experiments suggest that while people do free-ride, as Olson believed, they do so very much less than is commonly thought. Indeed, many people devote far more energy to politics than their 'rational' self-interest would justify.

As the science of Public Choice has matured, radical insights have given way to more infilling of the details and testing of the results. As we shall see in a later section, some recent theory and experimentation has actually called into question some of the early presumptions of Public Choice scholars, or has called for them to be substantially refined or revised.

Another trend is that the use of mathematics is increasing, though some scholars still maintain that the focus should be on explaining real-world politics and government, not on refining more abstruse models. And Public Choice is having a deeper and deeper impact on political science, whose practitioners are increasingly inclined to use the 'rational actor' approach.

In 1965, Buchanan and Tullock founded the Public Choice Society to exchange ideas among scholars working in this new field. A measure of the growth of Public Choice is that the society's annual meetings now attract hundreds of participants, and that similar societies have been established in Europe and the Far East. From its faltering early concepts, Public Choice has now become a field of very lively debate.

3 WHO NEEDS GOVERNMENT?

Some projects we cannot do alone. That is fine if we can recruit others to share the work and expense – and the benefits too, so that everyone thinks it worthwhile. A city family, for instance, might not be able to afford and maintain a holiday home on the coast. But if they chip in to the cost with others, and one family volunteers to decorate the house, another to furnish it, another to keep the lawn and garden trim, and another to keep it stocked with provisions, then it becomes a viable project that they can all enjoy.

The problem comes with 'public goods' – where other people can share the benefits, even if they make no contribution to the effort – because there is no incentive for anyone to contribute, when they can enjoy for free the fruits of other people's labours.

Examples of public goods cited by David Hume were dredging harbours and raising armies. Everyone benefits from the boost to commerce or the improved security; but why should anyone volunteer to pay for the dredging, or volunteer for the army, when they would get the same benefit by doing nothing? Another example, cited this time by Gordon Tullock, is London's once notorious smog. It was obvious that such pollution could be ended by people switching to smokeless fuel; but smokeless fuel was more expensive. So who would pay the extra cost, knowing that their own contribution to the overall result would be small – and that even if enough people switched that things did improve, non-switchers could simply 'free-ride' on the switchers' personal sacrifice?

The result of this 'public goods' problem is that potentially beneficial projects – such as improving security, or cleaning up the air – never happen, or are done inadequately. Some goods that are identified as public goods are often later found not to be so – for example, dredging a harbour could be financed by harbour fees charged to boats using the facility. But there remain many theoretical and practical cases of public goods, and we may well employ government to do the things that we deem important, but which the market does not deliver or delivers poorly. We vote, decide on the collective action, and then force everyone to share in it – banning their use of smoky fuels, for example, or taxing them to finance defence and public works.

This is why Public Choice scholars such as Buchanan and Tullock regard the state not as something 'organic', something that just grows, with a life and purposes of its own. Rather, they see government as simply a means by which rational, self-interested individuals combine to promote their personal interests through collective action.

The costs of decision-making

The question then becomes: what should be the rules for taking these collective decisions? In particular, what size of a majority is sufficient to justify forcing everyone to participate in a collective project?

It might seem that the ideal is unanimity – such that nobody has to be forced to participate, but everyone voluntarily agrees to contribute for mutual benefit. However, in today's large societies, getting millions of people to agree would involve major effort, and might well prove impossible. Also, if unanimity is required, any individual would be able to veto a proposal – and then free-ride if others went ahead by themselves and provided the 'public good' being debated.

But anything less than unanimity also has its downsides. Majority voting allows the majority to push through projects designed for their own benefit, which everyone else is then forced to accept or pay for. Indeed, such exploitation is very common. Compulsory taxes are imposed to fund government projects, activities or subsidies that minorities may resent paying for or even disapprove of bitterly. The majority often goes even farther, imposing its own values on the minority, prosecuting them for victimless lifestyle 'crimes' such as drug-taking, and otherwise infringing their basic liberties.

The higher the majority we set, the harder it is to reach agreement, but the lower the risk of minorities being exploited – or, as Buchanan and Tullock would put it, the higher the *decision-making costs* and the lower the *external costs*. Likewise, the lower the majority we set, the easier it will be to agree, but the greater is the risk of exploitation.

Finding the balance

Ideally we will find some majority rule where the total of the *decision-making costs* and *external costs* is minimised – a majority small enough to make agreement easy but large enough to make exploitation difficult.

Of course, the decision-making rule we normally rely on,

and which prevails in so many of the world's political systems, is simple majority voting – decisions are taken according to whatever more than half the public will vote for. But Public Choice scholars believe that the choice of a voting rule is extremely important, precisely because government decisions rest on coercion: the minority – which could be just under half the population – is forced to pay for what the majority want to do, and have to put up with the effects of the majority decision, no matter how strongly they might oppose it. So there is a trade-off: yes, we want collective decision-making to be easy; but we should also want to minimise the use of force on dissenters who may not benefit from the project the majority is demanding.

The best rule, then, may not be the simple majority rule that prevails in so many of the world's political systems. Common though it is, there is nothing magical about majority voting, according to Buchanan and Tullock. They point out that many other possible arrangements exist, including qualified majorities such as a two-thirds rule.

Indeed, we could well employ a variety of different voting rules, depending on the matter in hand. When the risk of being exploited is low, for example, people might agree to be bound by simple majority rule; but where the risk is high, they may insist on much larger majorities. The higher the *external costs*, in other words, the more *inclusive* should be the voting rule.

This is precisely why Wicksell favoured unanimous decisions on questions of taxation; and it is why Buchanan and Tullock argue that constitutions, which set all future voting rules, must be adopted unanimously.

Government failure

Before the rise of Public Choice, most economists supposed that government action could (and should) be used to correct 'market failure' problems such as the under-supply of public goods. But Public Choice scholars raised serious doubts about the wisdom of this assumption. The existence of 'market failure' does not necessarily mean that government action is any better. Public Choice reminds us that there is *government failure* too.

For example, no voting system truly reflects the different strengths of opinion of all the individuals involved. Governments cannot possibly know the preferences of all their electors, so can hardly claim to know what is in the 'public interest'. Different voting systems will throw up different answers. Meanwhile, majority systems expose the minority to damaging exploitation, and are burdened by the wasteful activity of rent seeking by special interest groups.

The market may be unable to deliver certain things, but government action – beset as it is with all these problems – is not necessarily an ideal way to deliver them either. Indeed, the problems that government intervention *creates* can be even more damaging than those it is intended to correct.

Public Choice scholars, then, accept that there may be a need for government action. But, they say, we need to be realistic about how government works. We need to look at the voting rules and how far we are prepared to force people to comply with whatever action is decided upon. And we need to weigh up whether government action, with all its faults, is actually the right way to try to do the important things that the market does not do adequately. Just because there are some useful things that the market does not deliver, it does not follow that more government intervention is the right answer.

Indivisibility of public goods

There is also the problem that public goods are all or nothing, as noted above in the case of harbour dredging. Should we dredge the harbour? Should we raise an army? Should we ban smoky fuel? The answer has to be yes or no: there is no in-between, and those in the minority are forced to accept the collective yes/no decision. Market goods, by contrast, are diverse: those who want black, blue, brown or red shoes can all have them at the same time, and in any style and quantity they choose, without having to force everyone else to go along with their preference. If we can find a way of providing certain types of public good by voluntary collective action, we might get closer to the kind of diversity we see in the market for private goods.

Furthermore, elections, the way that we express our preference on what collective action should prevail, occur only every few years. That contrasts very unfavourably with the market, where we are constantly choosing what we want, expressing our individual preferences through what we buy, every hour of every day.

In the market, moreover, we can take or leave any individual product from a vast and diverse array. We can buy peaches and apricots without being forced to buy beef and bacon at the same time, which is just as well if you happen to be a vegetarian. At elections, though, we do not choose individual projects, but vote on a whole supermarket basket of policies that could embrace issues as diverse as immigration, schools, healthcare, welfare, public expenditure, taxation and prisons. We may like some parts of the package, but hate others; unfortunately, we cannot pick and choose.

Expansionary pressure

Despite these shortcomings, there are still constant pressures to expand government activity. In the public debate, for example, the voices of groups with sharply focused interests – such as defence contractors or trade unionists – drown out those of the mass of voters, whose interests are much less specific. The concentrated interest groups have a powerful incentive to organise, raise funds and campaign for policies that will specifically benefit them. By contrast, the general public, with very diffused interests, have little motivation to put much effort into the public debate.

Another reason that government activity tends to expand is that the majority can pass off the cost of its decisions not just to the minority, but to generations yet unborn. Many public activities are not paid for out of the taxes of those who benefit from them, but are funded by public debt – which future generations will inherit. So people can vote themselves benefits such as higher pensions or better roads today, and yet shift their cost on to the taxpayers of tomorrow. Given this opportunity for 'time shifting', it is no wonder that so many people are keen for public services to expand.[1]

The expansionary pressure is boosted further by the 'you vote for my project and I will vote for yours' phenomenon of logrolling,

---

1   Some economists may point out that governments borrow to invest in assets that provide returns in the future, such as roads. Indeed, one of the 'golden rules' of the Labour government of 1997–2010 embraced exactly that principle. This reasoning is problematic, however. There is no general agreement about what constitutes investment; investment projects can themselves be determined by interested groups and have no long-term pay-off; and, in general, government spending and revenues are not hypothecated in this manner. In the end the 'golden rules' of the Labour government just fell into disrepute. More generally, Public Choice economics argues that interest groups can easily promote borrowing to finance current spending.

which seems to go hand in hand with democratic systems. When I worked at the US Congress, for example, I expressed surprise that the Food Stamp programme, a welfare measure, was tacked on to the end of the Farm Bill, which was mostly about farm subsidies. My colleagues rolled their eyes at my naivety: the rural Republicans, they explained, voted for the farm subsidies, and the urban Democrats voted for the welfare measure, so everyone benefited – except taxpayers, of course.

No direct link between choice and outcome

Public Choice points to yet another failure of the political system, that of *strategic* or *tactical voting*. In market transactions, you make your choice and you get the good or service that you want. In politics, you can express your choice in elections, but you may well end up with something you really hate.

For this reason, many people do not express their true preferences in elections, but vote tactically. They might not vote for their favoured party or option, but for some other that has a better chance of winning. If the Labour Party candidate has little prospect of winning in a UK parliamentary constituency, for example, Labour supporters may instead vote for the Liberal Democrat candidate in the hope of keeping out their Conservative arch-rivals.

This sends a false message to politicians and government officials, however, about what the electorate really want. It is hard enough to sum up the public mood from an election, when each person gets only one vote no matter how strongly they feel on an issue, and when electors' views often conflict. When many people are not even voting for what they believe in, the task becomes even harder. And when many electors decide, perfectly rationally, that their vote counts for so little that they would be wasting their time to research the issues – or even bother to vote at all – our supposedly democratic choices begin to look even less legitimate.

Interest groups, logrolling, voter ignorance, strategic voting, bundling, time shifting, coercion, monopoly, exploitation ... it is plain that government has failures of its own. As Buchanan and Tullock say, government is not something that we should get romantic about.

4 HOW TO WIN ELECTIONS

It has been said that if you like laws or sausages, you should never watch either being made. The quip sums up a Public Choice scholar's view of elections. The purpose of voting is to try somehow to translate the opinions of many individuals into one collective decision. But the decision that eventually emerges depends greatly on what particular electoral system is chosen. Moreover, every system has its own quirks – not just in terms of the mechanics of how it operates, but in terms of how it affects the way that voters and candidates behave. The political process is plainly not very pretty; and the final decision that emerges from it may be a much distorted reflection of what anyone actually wants.

Voting paradoxes in action

Indeed, as Condorcet pointed out, some systems could produce almost *any* result. Rock might lose to Paper, and Paper to Scissors, but Scissors would still be defeated by Rock. The outcome depends on how the election is managed. If there is someone who can set the order in which the votes are taken – say, the chair of a committee that has to choose between several options – that *agenda-setter* can rig the order in which the votes are taken in order to ensure that his or her own preferences prevail, regardless of what other people want.

As Duncan Black calculated – and recent analysis confirms – the more options that are on offer, and the more electors there are voting, the more severe this *cycling* paradox becomes, making it of particular importance in the large and complex political systems of today.

For instance, it is of real importance in the election of US presidents, where the candidates are narrowed down to two or three by means of a series of primary elections. It can also be seen in the election of presidents in France, where the leading candidates from a first round of voting go into a second-round run-off: thus in 2002, the National Front leader Jean-Marie Le Pen came a close second in the first ballot of sixteen candidates, only to lose by a landslide to Jacques Chirac in the run-off, while the socialists, a very close third, did not get on the second-round ballot paper at all. A different voting system could have produced a different result entirely. If there had been fewer left-wing candidates, then the socialist might have beaten the national socialist to second place. The National Front voters – whose candidate would have been eliminated – could have voted for the socialist instead of for Chirac and the socialist could have won.

Third parties often complain about the voting paradox. Britain's Liberal Democrats, for example, would probably win a majority in any two-party election, since Labour supporters would choose them in preference to the Conservatives, and Conservatives would choose them over Labour. But when, as is usual, all three parties are in contention, the Liberal Democrats generally lag in third place.

Other voting systems

Much of the early work on Public Choice focused on the single-member, first-past-the-post systems that prevailed in the UK and the USA. In these systems, the country is divided into geographical constituencies; several candidates compete for each, and in each the candidate with the largest number of votes is elected to the legislature. That does not mean that winning candidates will secure a majority of the votes cast. Often, if the votes are split between many candidates, the winner is elected on the support of only a small minority of those voting.

Such concerns have led to the adoption of *proportional representation* systems in many other countries, such as those of continental Europe. In many of these systems, the political parties draw up lists of their preferred candidates, and electors vote for the party rather than for the individual. The seats are then allocated between the parties on the basis of the number of votes polled by each party. This can lead to minority party candidates being more fairly represented in the legislature. But it also puts considerable power in the hands of the party bosses who draw up the candidate lists, giving them greater leverage over the agenda than in single-member systems, where representatives have more allegiance to their own electors.

Another issue is that proportional representation frequently produces minority or coalition governments, which require compromise between different parties – producing a hybrid policy programme that nobody actually voted for. The same criticism is made of *alternative-vote* systems, where only one member is elected per constituency, but voters rank the candidates in order of preference. The lowest-rank candidates are eliminated and their second-preference votes are reallocated between the remaining candidates until a majority winner emerges. The candidate who wins might be the one who is least offensive to slightly more than 50 per cent of voters rather than one who has strong support from slightly less than 50 per cent of voters. Alternative vote systems and first-past-the-post produce different outcomes but neither one nor the other can be said to be unequivocally better.

Rational ignorance

Voting demands a little time and effort from the elector. It is not just the modest time and effort of making your way to the polling station and filling in the ballot form. There is also the much greater time and effort that is needed to inform yourself about the candidates and their policies so that you can make a choice.

Given what is at stake, this is a potentially huge task for electors. After all, they are choosing a government that may run perhaps half of the nation's economy for the next four or five years. The question of who should be given a five-year monopoly on the entire production of defence, education, welfare, policing or healthcare, and on the regulation of industry, finance, transport and public safety – plus much else – seems worthy of a great deal of thought and research by the electors who appoint them.

Yet any single elector's choice is unlikely to make a difference to the election outcome. Even if it does, it may not deliver their chosen result: an honest vote for a losing Labour candidate, for example, may deny the Liberal Democrats the one vote that would allow them to beat the Conservatives that the elector hates.

Voters face another uncertainty, too. In a marketplace, prices are not always transparent, and the quality of products is not always clear. Generally speaking, though, if you buy a cup of coffee, you know what it is going to cost you, and you know pretty clearly what you will get in return. You pay the whole cost, and you get the whole benefit. But in politics, the costs and benefits are spread among many people. If you vote for a programme such as public healthcare, you do not necessarily know what it will end up costing you personally, or precisely how much of the benefit will come to you. You might get a better job and move into a higher tax bracket and find yourself paying more; or you may never get sick enough to need the service.

This uncertainty about costs and benefits, and the minuscule chance that your vote will have a real and predictable effect on the election, give rise to the *rational ignorance* described by Anthony Downs. The thought may be unsettling for democrats but, logically, electors are quite right: it is simply not worth their time and effort to become well informed on the candidates or their policies.

The vote motive

Indeed, it is not obvious why rational people bother to vote at all; perhaps it is something we feel we should do, however slight its effect, like cheering our favourite football team. But the fact is that people do vote – and in ways they hope will promote their own interests, according to Public Choice.

Those who run political parties, meanwhile, are pursuing interests of their own. According to early Public Choice scholars such as Black and Downs, their goal is to gather votes, and get their party elected. That is the source of the power and status they value. This *vote motive* is what shapes their political positioning: they choose policies because they think they will win, and not necessarily because they think they are right.

There is undoubtedly a great deal in this view. We have all seen political parties adopt – and ditch – policies on the strength of the opinion polls alone. More recent Public Choice scholars have argued, however, that political parties do not actually drift so freely from one policy to another. Normally, they have some broad ideology, and adopt policies that are generally consistent with that world view. Indeed, they would lose credibility if they suddenly abandoned their principles or their policies for immediate electoral advantage. And having an ideological stance could itself be a vote-garnering device: if voters are indeed rationally ignorant, the parties will be able to attract them only by having some broad label or approach that even uninformed voters will recognise and support.

The drift to the middle

Another point made originally by Duncan Black is that vote-seeking parties will tend to bid for the middle ground – his *median voter theorem*.

Take some simple issue such as how much we should spend on defence. Public Choice scholars call these *one-dimensional* issues, since people's choices lie somewhere on a single scale, ranging between nothing and a great deal.

A few people will say we should spend nothing at all on defence, and a few will say we should spend much more than we do at present. But, like the shape of a bell, most people are likely to bunch around some point in the middle. To use the jargon again, their preferences are *single-peaked*. Not only are there more voters in the middle but if a party pitches its policy closer to where the voters bunch it is still likely to pick up those voters at one of the extremes. The rational vote-gathering strategy for an extreme party is therefore to move towards the centre, hoping that its more extreme followers will stay with it while simultaneously gathering up some of the large mass of moderate voters. Indeed, the nearer to the centre that any party moves, the more advantage it has over any that are farther out.

The result, said Black, is that political parties converge on the centre of opinion, trying to position themselves close to the 'median voter'. This view has a great deal of truth in it: electors in countries such as the UK and the USA often complain that there is 'no difference' between the parties. But, nevertheless, this simple idea has been challenged, and indeed largely abandoned, in recent times for a variety of reasons.

Firstly, it may work for a discrete, one-dimensional, single-peaked issue. But not when there are many, complicated, inter-related issues, where opinion may be split between many 'peaks'. It also supposes that parties know what voters are thinking and will blithely reposition themselves to win votes – and that voters are well informed enough to vote on the basis of that reposi-tioning, and trust that the parties are actually committed to deliv-ering their new-found policy.

When things are more true to life – say there are two major issues and three parties in contention – the positioning geometry gets much more complex. Then, it turns out, a party that moves away from the centre – though not too far – might well pick up valuable support from each of the other two. So we should expect greater differences between parties in a three-party system.

But even this is oversimplified. In reality, parties themselves are coalitions of activists who have different, competing interests, making it quite likely that the policy package they present to the public will include unpopular as well as popular measures: so voters might be torn between them. While there may well be some truth in the median voter theorem, it seems that real politics is simply more complex.

The myth of the rational voter

Even if the political parties are not such opportunistic vote-chasers as Black and other early Public Choice scholars portrayed them, it is still unwise to be too optimistic about the political process. In 2007 the US economist Bryan Caplan challenged the standard view that voters were reasonable people who could be trusted to cast their votes responsibly in elections. On the contrary, he said, they suffer from a number of irrational biases – biases which they can indulge because they know that the cost will not fall on them but will be spread across the whole population.

In the first place, voters hate job losses. So they vote for subsidies to farming and other industries, forgetting that technological and productivity improvements mean that this same labour would be better employed elsewhere. Voters are not necessarily good economists, so they do not see the second-round effects of good and bad economic policy. Secondly, says Caplan, voters are biased against foreigners, seeing them as a threat to domestic jobs, rather than welcoming the benefits of free trade. Thirdly, they overestimate the problems in the economy, rather than recognising that, over the long term, things are generally improving. Fourthly, they underestimate the benefits of the market mechanism and overestimate the effectiveness of political initiatives.

So perhaps we have to put *democratic failure* alongside

government failure. As we shall see, it is certainly true that government decisions may be distorted because of the voting system, or because of the self-interest of politicians and bureaucrats, or because well-organised interest groups dominate the public debate. But even if the voting system efficiently reflects public opinion, and even if politicians and bureaucrats faithfully carry out the public's wishes, the resulting public action could still be irrational, simply because the voters are irrational. There are varying theories here but all of them lead in the same direction – government is not necessarily well suited to dealing with what are often called 'market failures'. Politicians and officials may know full well what works and what should be done – allowing loss-making businesses to close down, for example – but may still find themselves conceding to voters' irrational biases and doing things that they know are ineffective or counterproductive, such as subsidising those loss-making industries. As has been noted, like making sausages, making laws remains an ugly business.

5 THE TYRANNY OF THE MINORITIES

Market transactions are voluntary: either side can walk away from the bargain if they do not like the terms on offer. But politics has to be coercive: once the collective decision has been taken, everyone must abide by it, even if they are unhappy about it. And if they try to evade the collective agreement – by not paying their taxes, for example – the state uses its authority to force them.

Force and the threat of force are never desirable, even if the cause is just. But an even more disquieting feature of majority rule is the possibility that the majority could use its power to coerce the minority quite unjustly, imposing high taxes on them or extinguishing their freedoms – all backed up by state power.

Things are actually even more disturbing than this 'sheep and two wolves' problem, however. Under majority voting, not only can the majority exploit the minority: it is even possible for small, organised *minorities* to get together and impose their will on the broad, unorganised *majority*. And this is particularly true in the election of representatives to a legislature.

Concentrated and diffused interests

It has long been obvious that special interest groups campaign vigorously in pursuit of their own interests. But Mancur Olson and William H. Riker were able to study this phenomenon in much more depth by applying to it the principles of Public Choice economics.

Once again, Public Choice assumes that members of such groups – tomato growers or opera companies, say – will seek to protect and promote their shared interest. Indeed, as Olson noted, they have a strong incentive to organise themselves politically. In the first place, they have a great deal to gain (or lose) when collective decisions go for (or against) them. And because they are small and homogeneous, it is relatively easy for them to organise.

The opposite is true with large groups, such as consumers or taxpayers. They have little incentive to throw their energy into campaigning: since they are so numerous, the impact of collective decisions on each individual is widely spread and therefore small. Being so diverse, they are also difficult to organise; and many people may figure that they could make scant difference to a joint lobbying effort anyway.

The result is that small groups with *concentrated interests* may be much more active, vocal and effective participants in collective decision-making than much larger groups with only *diffused interests*. While a ban on imported tomatoes, say, is of keen interest to tomato growers, it means just a minuscule loss of choice for consumers; similarly, a grant to an opera house might double the revenues of the company, yet add only a few pennies to anyone's tax bill.

But the pennies mount up. With potentially huge numbers of minority interests all campaigning to win special benefits at the expense of the broad majority, it should be no surprise if we end up with more regulations, more subsidies, higher taxes and a bigger government than any of us really want. Once again, it seems there is good reason to be pessimistic about the political process.

Interest group politics

Lobby groups know that their particular interests may have little traction with the general voting public or the politicians who represent them. So they often dress up their demands in 'public interest' language. Tomato growers might argue that an import ban would save us from low-quality or diseased tomatoes from abroad, and would boost farm employment and prosperity at home; opera companies might argue that a thriving opera culture helps uplift us or makes our country a more attractive destination for tourists.

Back in 1776, Adam Smith wisely counselled that such arguments should be 'long and carefully examined, not only with the most scrupulous, but with the most suspicious attention'. Nevertheless, the fact that small lobby groups make a disproportionately loud noise in the public debate – and are likely to be better informed on the particular subject than are most other people – means that politicians in turn give their arguments disproportionate attention, and find it easier to give in to their demands even if it harms the less vocal majority. Indeed, since interest groups have an incentive to raise lobbying funds, there is also the enticing prospect of campaign contributions for the politicians who support them. As the Public Choice approach reminds us, politicians have their own interests too. That is one reason why representative systems are so easily and commonly dominated by quite small interest group movements.

However loud the public campaigning, though, the real lobbying may well take place behind closed doors. As Olson noted, the opaque nature of this process works to the advantage of the lobbyists and the politicians, who can secretly trade mutual support; and the established lobby groups and the incumbent politicians are the ones who probably gain most. But the process works against the interests of consumers and taxpayers, who are not represented in these private discussions.

Organisational problems

Very small interest groups whose members have highly similar interests are likely to be the easiest to organise. But since they have so few members, they may struggle to raise enough campaign funds to buy enough administrative support and public relations expertise to lobby effectively and make their voice heard.

Larger groups have a larger pool of members from which to raise money and draw activists, but the problems of free-riding grow with size. Members may leave it to others to stump up the funds and do the work, knowing that if the group's lobbying proves successful, they will benefit, whether they made any contribution to it or not – in other words, larger groups have a 'free-rider' problem.

Interest groups may be able to avoid this free-rider problem if they can restrict the benefits of their lobbying to their own members. Professional associations, trade unions, producer bodies and others may get politicians to give special recognition to their members, who pay campaign subscriptions to them. The future benefits that they win from the political process, such as monopolies or tax privileges, can then be restricted to the recognised group. Doctors and lawyers, for example, all benefit from licensing arrangements that allow them to limit their numbers, raise their charges, and prevent work going to 'unqualified' competitors.

Coalition-building

Even if small groups are easier to organise, it still helps to have some critical mass in the political debate. But in representative democracies, not a great deal is needed: Buchanan and Tullock calculated that a group able to marshal just over a quarter of the voters in a large electorate could dominate an apathetic and unorganised majority. Imagine, for example, a country in which there are 100 constituencies, each with 10,000 voters. To have a ruling majority in the legislature, a party or interest group has to get only a simple majority of voters – 5,001 – in a simple majority of the seats – 51. Though the electorate is 1,000,000 strong, a mere 255,051 voters are needed for victory.

Of course, most interest groups do not have so many members, nor can they calculate their vote requirements so finely. But if most electors do not bother to vote, or if their vote splits evenly, even smaller minorities can sway the result.

One way in which minorities can increase their voting strength, and therefore their dominance over representative systems, is to form *coalitions* with other minorities – either with those who share their broad stance or with those who are prepared to support their cause in return for support of their own.

Exactly how this coalition-building works depends on the nature of the electoral system – another case in which the decision-making institutions are important. First-past-the-post systems commonly produce pre-election coalitions in which interested individuals and groups sink their differences and join one of the dominant parties or where minority parties sink their differences and create alliances that are potentially large enough to challenge the incumbents. Alternatively, they may merely form electoral pacts to exploit tactical voting opportunities, declining to put up candidates in areas where their pact partners have a better chance of winning.

In continental Europe and other legislatures where proportional systems and multi-party politics prevail, however, coalitions are more likely to be formed *after* the election, in the legislature. Once the election returns are in, and the voting strength of the different parties is clear, party managers know what numbers they need to put together in order to form a majority and can make informed judgements about which alliance partners might best deliver.

William H. Riker explored many of these issues, explaining many features of coalitions, such as why 'grand coalitions' that embrace many different parties or interest groups tend to be short-lived. Subsequently, economists have applied more sophisticated game theory to such questions, with interesting results.

The behaviour of coalitions

The key questions, of course, are which parties are likely to form a coalition, and how long is a coalition likely to last. Riker concluded that rather than having broad coalitions from which different interest groups might peel off at inopportune moments, the optimum strategy must be to construct a *minimum winning coalition*, large enough to dominate the agenda without being so large as to be unstable.

While this theory looks as plausible as any other, the reality is that it accounts for less than half of the post-war governments in multi-party European countries. Nor does it explain the existence of the minority governments that occur often in Europe and elsewhere. For those, the Dutch social scientist and expert

on coalitions Peter van Roozendaal may have a better explanation. In his view, it is easier for smaller parties to enter alliances
with central parties, rather than with other smaller parties at the
opposite end of the political spectrum; so a large central party will
have a pivotal position in any coalition. Given that dominance, it
may prefer to go it alone and form a minority government, relying
on shifting alliances with other parties to either side, as and when
it needs their support.

Minority governments tend to be short-lived, however. That
may be because, in reality, politics is not about simple one-dimensional, single-peak issues where public opinion bunches at some
point on a single scale. Political issues are often *multidimensional*
and *multi-peak* – involving complex, numerous, interrelated and
changing questions where public opinion is divided many ways.
That makes it much harder to maintain a stable coalition.

From coalitions to vote trading

Public Choice and game theory have come up with other interesting insights on the subject of coalitions, such as the suggestion
that they are less permanent when social mobility is high. If there
is permanent social division, coalitions can be built and main-
tained on the strength of it; but if the social sands are shifting,
there is a less sure foundation.

Theory also suggests that coalitions are more difficult to form
and maintain as the number of the electorate increases. And both
theory and observation suggest that it is much easier to form
stable coalitions where there is a more uniform population. These
insights might explain why small, socially conservative and homogeneous countries – such as those in Scandinavia – generally have

more stable politics than large, mobile and ethnically diverse countries.

But how far will the silent majority remain silent when faced with the tyranny of the minorities in representative systems? After all, they are exposed to potentially high burdens in the shape of the regulations and higher taxes that organised coalitions can impose on them – not to mention the cost of all this lobbying on the economy as a whole. Sadly, the fact that consumers and taxpayers are rarely organised as an effective political force – together with the growth of government programmes, the proliferation of politically active pressure groups and the expansion of the lobbying industry – suggests that the answer might be that the majority's silence could last a long time.

6 THE MARKET FOR VOTES: LOGROLLING

There is more to interest-group politics than forming one-off coalitions to build a majority on a single issue. Politics is a continual process, with a variety of different issues coming up over time – a state of affairs that gives wide scope for individuals and groups to gain from exchanging support between each other.

Again, the process starts with a group that feels intensely about some issue – the need for better roads in its own locality, say. It makes a simple bargain with other such groups: you vote to improve our roads today, and we will vote to improve yours some time soon.

In the USA, such vote trading is known as *logrolling*. The expression probably derives from the old practice of neighbours assisting each other to move felled timber, which is difficult to do alone.

Implicit and explicit logrolling

An agreement to exchange votes on separate legislative measures, as in the roads example, is called *explicit logrolling*. It is common in democratic bodies, such as committees and legislatures, where votes are easily traded and – since both partners need to know that the other is delivering the bargain – easily observed. It does not work so well in secret ballots, or between large groups that cannot easily discipline their members.

Another mechanism, *implicit logrolling*, is where the different groups bundle their various proposals into a package before they are voted on. So voters or legislators who feel very strongly about one measure also end up voting for other people's measures too. This kind of vote trading is common when party election manifestos or legislative proposals are being put together. The US president Dwight Eisenhower, for example, packaged his interstate highway plans so that they benefited a majority of states: in voting for better roads in their own state, members of Congress found themselves voting for the whole network.

Implicit logrolling has many benefits for legislators. By packaging their special interest measure with those of others, they can attract greater support for it, without accepting responsibility for the whole package. They can simply explain that it was a compromise: to improve the roads in their own locality (say), they were forced to go along with the other measures too. The Food Stamps and Farm Bill arrangement is a perfect example.

It is therefore no surprise that logrolling is a significant part of the democratic process. But, unlike in implicit logrolling, where the package to be voted on may be worked out in deals behind closed doors, the vote trading in explicit logrolling is at least transparent: everyone can see how votes are being traded.

Even so, some 'explicit' vote trading is not actually so explicit. Where a number of issues are coming up, as they do in legislatures all the time, there is quite often only an unspoken assumption of mutual support. Legislators will vote for colleagues' projects in the hope and expectation that those colleagues will remember the favour and return it by voting for their favoured measure when the time comes. Indeed, the process is so subtle that the representatives themselves do not even realise they are doing it.

Gordon Tullock cited the case of a British Member of Parliament who was shocked by the idea that votes were traded and denied it happened – but then went on to explain how he arm-twisted other MPs to support his measures, fully expecting them to arm-twist him to support subsequent measures of their own.

The prevalence of logrolling

Explicit logrolling is very common across representative politics. It is particularly open in the USA, where the federal system means that members of Congress are *expected* to fight for benefits to their own state or district, and national party policy comes second. It is not so obvious in European countries where national party discipline is stronger, but it is very significant at European Union level, where bargains have to be made between EU countries.

New EU institutions, for example, are assigned to one country after another (the investment bank in Luxembourg, the central bank in Frankfurt, the parliament in Brussels *and* Strasbourg) and top posts are passed around the member states.

In everyday European Union decisions too, the requirement of unanimity on certain policy issues once meant that individual countries could easily threaten to block agreement. The difficulty of making decisions under the unanimity rule led to it being largely abandoned for most issues by the EU, in favour of qualified majority voting (though this still allows a fair amount of scope for logrolling).

Under the unanimity rule, the ability of any EU member state to veto any proposal was a useful longstop against its vital interests being overridden by others. But the veto threat also gave each member state enormous vote-trading opportunities that could be used to extract costly concessions from the majority; and the willingness of almost every member state to extract such concessions led to some very lopsided policies and put constant pressure on the budget. All round, in fact, EU decision-making processes have provided a particularly rich source of material for modern Public Choice scholars.

Implicit logrolling is strong at many levels, particularly in the formation of parties and their election programmes. Parties are by nature assemblies of different interests who agree to support each other so as to build an activist group of credible size and strength. The fact that parties often suffer internal disagreements and splits is evidence of this trading partnership. And when they draw up their election programmes too, parties enter into vote trading with the electorate. They will shape their policy packages so as to woo strong groups at the election. If the policies they adhere to most deeply are not popular with the public, they will balance them with popular policies that will go down well with voters, even if party members themselves are not much moved by them. Then, if voters want the popular policies, they must accept the unpopular ones alongside them as part of the package on offer.

The same occurs in ballot initiatives, a kind of local referendum where US voter groups can put forward policy initiatives such as raising loans or taxes to build a new road or school. Often, several different policies will be contained in the same initiative – the aim being to induce minorities to vote for the whole package in order to get the specific items that are dear to them, even though they may be cool on many of the other elements.

Logrolling in the legislature

Once in office, political leaders also engage in logrolling as they decide on the policy measures that will go to the legislature. Cabinet ministers may agree to support legislative proposals that will benefit a colleague, even if they do not much like the measure, on the (often unspoken) presumption that the colleague will in turn support them in cabinet when the situation is reversed. And almost every measure that gets to the legislature is itself likely to become the object of implicit logrolling, as its promoters make concessions or add details that will buy the support of minorities and so ensure its smooth passage.

Occasionally, this process can reach absurd proportions. One example is the 2008 emergency measure to bail out troubled US banks. When first presented to the US Congress it was just a few pages long. But legislators knew that because the Bill was so critical and simply had to pass, they could make all kinds of demands in exchange for their support. After many rounds of vote trading, the bill eventually emerged at 451 pages, and contained many concessions that had nothing to do with its original purpose, but which bought off numerous interest groups. These concessions included tax breaks for motorsports complexes and for fishing interests that had been harmed by the Exxon Valdez oil spill twenty years earlier, subsidies for people who cycle to work, $148 million in tax reliefs for wool fabric producers, $192 million in excise tax rebates for the rum industry, and a $2 million tax benefit for makers of wooden arrows for children.

In contrast to this, in the UK, the emergency measures to bail out the banks went through parliament in three days. This is because of the whipping system, strong parliamentary discipline and the fact that the government is largely drawn from parliament in the UK. MPs are expected to vote as directed and to support the party line across all aspects of a piece of legislation. Logrolling is therefore more difficult in the UK – though not impossible.

The effects of logrolling

Although logrolling sounds like a distasteful activity, it can sometimes be both beneficial and efficient, say Public Choice scholars. It is efficient in that it exposes the different strengths of feeling on an issue, which a simple one-person-one-vote referendum would not. Minority groups that feel passionately about an issue can make sure, through vote trading – or even by explicitly buying votes for cash – that their passion is properly acknowledged.

To take an everyday example, imagine three student roommates voting on whether to buy, jointly, a television that none could afford on their own. One is intensely keen on getting a television, but the other two are each very marginally against. If a vote is taken, the TV will be rejected; but this does not reflect the intensity of feelings within the group. If the pro-TV student paid one of the others to vote yes, or offered to return the favour in some future vote, the intensity of feelings is reflected and the group will buy the TV.

Vote trading can also be positive in cases where the benefits to a locality of a project (such as a new road) may exceed its cost – meaning that the project should go ahead – but where it is blocked because the rest of the electorate are reluctant to pay higher taxes for something they will never use. Though such projects may be worthwhile, it is only vote trading that will get them through a democratic system.

To illustrate, Gordon Tullock gives the example of nine voters facing a measure that will cost them each £1 in tax but will confer a benefit of £15 on one of them. With eight losers and only one winner, the vote will go against, even though the £15 total benefit exceeds the £9 total cost. But if each of the eight stands to benefit from similar initiatives, it makes sense for them to support each other's projects, and all will benefit.

But logrolling can produce negative results too. Suppose the benefit is only £7 while the tax is still £1. Here, each voter could assemble a majority by trading votes on four other projects, costing the voter just £5 in total for a £7 personal gain. Then, each project would go ahead despite the fact that the total cost of each was £9 while the total benefit of each was only £7.

Other problems of logrolling

In practice, this negative effect is very common: logrolling subjects the taxpayers of a large democracy to the cost of very large numbers of logrolling trades that buy political support but do not justify their financial costs. The USA even has a name for it – *pork barrel politics* – in which massively wasteful projects are agreed in this way. The fact that representatives are keen to buy off strident or blocking minorities just adds to the potential cost and waste. On the one hand, logrolling allows the strength of feeling of a minority on an issue to be reflected in a way that is impossible using a simple ballot. On the other hand, this, itself, leads to more opportunities for minorities to organise and make effective their support for projects that may benefit them but impose widely dispersed costs upon the community.

When there are many minorities to be bought off, legislative proposals can grow into massive omnibus measures, as the 2008 bailout Bill did. In fact, they can grow so large that legislators may not have time even to read them, never mind understand them. And every time such a measure goes through, it creates many new projects, leading to an expansion – indeed an over-expansion – of government.

At best, then, logrolling is part of a democratic, participative and consultative process that gives minorities a say in their democracy. But it is also often opaque, dominated by political interests and likely to load costs on the general public. At worst, it can degenerate into outright corruption, where votes are sold for cash or favours. Sometimes it is hard to know where the line should be drawn.

Containing logrolling

Though logrolling is widely prevalent, it can be contained. Referenda on single issues, being single rather than serial votes, make logrolling relatively difficult. A two-chamber legislature, particularly if each house is elected on a different basis, also marginally discourages logrolling because it increases the difficulty of vote trading, while making its results less certain to predict. A presidential veto adds even more to the difficulty and uncertainty of logrolling.

Nevertheless, even though the US constitution has all these elements, logrolling remains a major part of American politics. It seems particularly strong in the House of Representatives, where members face election every two years and represent relatively small districts. This places them under constant electoral pressure, which makes constant vote trading and coalition-building critical to their re-election. Presidents, who face an election every four years, also have to be quite effective logrollers. But there is less logrolling in the Senate, where members are elected every six years, and the electoral pressure is therefore much less.

Perhaps the only lasting antidote to logrolling, however, is a set of restraints that keep the size of governments, and therefore the potential gains from logrolling, small.

7 POLITICAL PROFITS: RENT SEEKING

Like so many of the crucial insights in Public Choice theory, the idea of *rent seeking* was first outlined (in 1967) by Gordon Tullock, although the phrase itself was coined by Anne Krueger some years later.

Most ordinary people think of *rent* as a payment made to the owner of land or other resources – without the owner necessarily having to do much work for it. Economists have a more technical definition, which defines *economic rent* as returns in excess of normal competitive levels; but the ordinary way of thinking does somehow sum up the essence of rent seeking.

In market situations, a supplier who faces no competition – say, the sole grocer in a village – can charge higher prices (and provide a worse service) than one who does. But these high profits attract the attention of other potential grocers, who are free to open a shop and compete with the original. The result of such competition is that the former monopolist has to cut prices and improve service to stay in business.

In political situations, things are very different. Opportunities to make excess profits occur only where the political authorities create them, by making it hard or impossible for new market entrants to come in and compete. A good example is the regulation of New York taxis, which severely limits their number to 13,000 – which is less than half the number that operated even during the Great Depression years. Because new competition is outlawed, taxi drivers make more money and New Yorkers pay more and wait longer for taxis than they otherwise would. A New York taxi licence has recently changed hands for $1 million, thus illustrating the size of the rents that are now being protected.

Governments commonly grant *themselves* monopolies over the provision of services such as education or the postal system. In earlier times, monarchs granted their friends and courtiers explicit monopolies over goods ranging from salt to soap, candles, starch, paper and sweet wine. Things today are more subtle, but government licensing of professions (such as those of accountants, dentists and even hairdressers and manicurists), together with quotas and tariffs on imported goods and planning rules on the use of land, serves to reduce and stifle competition and deliver monopoly profits – 'rent' – to the various favoured groups.

The lure of rent seeking

Rent seeking is the attempt by particular groups to persuade governments to grant them these sorts of valuable monopolies or legal privileges. If their rent seeking is successful, such benefits could add up to a substantial transfer of wealth to these privileged groups from the general public. Consumers and taxpayers lose financially as a result of the monopoly prices, but also lose in terms of the reduced choice and lower quality that they have to endure too.

Tullock pointed out that the potential gains from successful rent seeking are in fact so substantial that it makes perfect sense for groups to spend a great deal of time, effort and money in trying to capture them. It could be worth billions to domestic carmakers, for instance, if they managed to persuade legislators to impose quotas or tariffs on foreign car imports. So it should be no surprise that they are willing to spend millions lobbying to achieve precisely that result.

But as Tullock noted, all this expensive lobbying activity is unproductive, and a pure loss to the economy. The time, effort, money, skill and entrepreneurial activity of many talented people are wasted on it. Rent-seeking activity produces nothing of value to the community. All it does is determine which monopoly privileges will be granted to which interest groups.

Tullock's observation that rent-seeking groups would spend – or in terms of the community as a whole, waste – huge resources on trying to tilt law-making in their own favour came as a real blow to the 'welfare economics' ideas of the mainstream economics profession. They believed that collective choices could correct 'market failure' and promote the general welfare; but they gave little thought to the real-world processes of collective decision-making, and assumed that policy would be made rationally in the general interest by enlightened public officials. Tullock's insight made it clear, however, that, far from the public policy process being superior to the market, rent seeking massively distorts public decisions, and in turn distorts markets and reduces competition in ways that benefit certain groups but substantially injure the general community.

Costs and distortions

The ways in which the effects of rent seeking impose costs on other people are many. Suppose, for example, that a high-tech industry group successfully lobbies for tax breaks on research and development. The idea might be presented as a way of keeping the country at the leading edge of technology and stimulating the development of new high-tech products that people in other countries will want to buy. And it may indeed have some such effect.

But, equally, it might simply make it cheaper for companies to do the same research and development that they would have done anyway. The tax break also distorts the tax system, drawing resources into research and development and away from other places – places where those resources might have been used more productively. The prospect of lower taxes might also induce firms to classify activities as 'research and development' that really are not, solely in order to get the benefit.

Meanwhile, the fact that the Treasury is not collecting revenue from these activities means that, to maintain its spending levels, the government will have to raise more money from elsewhere. So other people's taxes will have to rise. Not only is this bad for them; higher rates of tax also encourage more people to (legally) avoid or (illegally) evade their taxes. And the higher the tax rates, the more people will campaign for special loopholes or concessions of their own, in order to keep their burden down. If they succeed, that further distorts economic activity, drawing resources out of customer service and into tax avoidance, setting off the same cycle again.

Similar problems occur when groups successfully campaign for a subsidy – say, government grants to biofuel producers. Again, that draws more economic activity into biofuel production. The additional demand for crops that can be made into fuel will raise their price, and food prices rise, adding to the cost of living, which affects poorest people hardest. Once again, the costs are

dispersed and opaque and the benefits concentrate(
interest groups with well-defined interests.

Or again, groups may seek to benefit themsel
the state welfare system. If there are cash benefits to low-income
households, for example, those just above the income cut-off level
could make themselves much better off by campaigning to raise
the cut-off level. Others might try to make themselves worse off –
or appear worse off – than they really are, so as to qualify.

Counting the cost

As the Nobel economist Milton Friedman noted, building a
factory potentially adds to public wealth; buying a New York taxi
medallion does not. And the larger the size of the public sector, or
the more complicated the tax or regulatory structure, the greater
the opportunities for rent seeking – so the larger this potential
loss becomes.

Companies, individuals and groups are likely to be prepared
to invest almost as much in rent seeking as the 'rent' that they will
get if they succeed. Rent seeking has a cost that draws resources
from other parts of the economy – often involving highly articulate,
educated and productive people. As a result of this cost, as well as
the economic welfare loss from successful rent seeking, the total
cost of the activity can grow to be enormous. One study in the early
2000s estimated interest-group spending on rent seeking in the
USA at several hundred million dollars. And another thing that adds
to the bill is that rent seeking is a gamble, which may or may not pay
off; and like many gamblers, rent seekers actually end up spending
more on the effort than they actually get back, even if successful.

The financial costs that rent seeking imposes on the rest of the public have another corrosive effect too. If people figure that their earnings, savings and capital earned through their own hard work can be prised from them (in taxes or monopoly prices) by rent seekers, they will be less willing to work hard and save in the first place. They will invest less in wealth creation, firms will be starved of finance, output will be lower and once again the general public will be worse off.

Political costs

Rent seeking also corrupts the political process. The prospect of extracting large benefits through rent seeking encourages groups to trade votes and support in order to make it happen.

The deep interest that rent seekers have in the concessions that will benefit them, and the time and energy that they are prepared to invest to capture them, helps explain why lobbying is such a big industry and why politicians end up granting so many monopolies, regulations and concessions. It also explains why such privileges tend to remain in place long after it is plainly obvious that they are inappropriate and inefficient, and that reform is needed.

The larger the power of the state, the more opportunities there are for rent seeking and the greater the power enjoyed by politicians as interest groups lobby them for favours. Politicians gain not just from the status that comes from being able to grant privileges to rent seekers who lobby them, but also from their ability to threaten adverse rulings on others. On occasion this power may lead to outright corruption, with politicians and officials granting special privileges to particular interest groups in return for cash or personal favours, and putting legal obstacles in the way of those who do not support them.

The huge potential gains of rent seeking, both to rent seekers and to politicians, and the imbalance between the concentrated interest of the minority gainers and the powerlessness of the majority public, might make one wonder why rent seeking has not become endemic in democratic systems. Unfortunately, the evidence is that it probably has.

8 PAYDAY FOR POLITICIANS

Why do we need legislators – all those representatives and parliamentarians that we love to hate so much? The main reason is straightforward – practicality. The sheer number of collective choices facing advanced countries every day would make it far too difficult and exhausting to expect everyone to turn out and vote on every issue. Nor would the general public even have the time and interest to research and form opinions on all those issues.

Accordingly we delegate the business of understanding the issues, forming judgements and taking decisions to a smaller, more manageable group – our professional legislators. We rely on their diligence, and their judgement, to represent our views and to take decisions on our behalf. That means decisions can be made with much less expenditure of time, effort and money.

Legislators and us

But do legislators perfectly represent our opinions? Academic economists may have assumed so, but most ordinary people (and politicians themselves) would be much less naive. In fact, say Public Choice scholars, legislators are no different from the rest of us: they have their own interests and opinions that inevitably affect their decisions.

The principles of Public Choice apply in legislatures just as much as they do at elections. In multi-party systems in particular, different parties may have to bargain and form coalitions in the legislature. Interest groups exert direct lobbying pressure on legislators, sometimes including vital financial support. And logrolling is a big factor in almost every legislature.

So we should not expect legislators' interests to coincide at all perfectly with those of their electors. Indeed, the people who are keenest to get into power are often those who want to exploit it for their own benefit, or for the benefit of their friends and factions, rather than to promote more general public interests. True, the public can restrain their politicians by voting them out at elections; but this control is very weak. Elections are infrequent, people will be voting for a bundle of different policies, and those who can dictate the key election issues, or set the date of the election, have a powerful influence on the outcome. Electors, meanwhile, know that their own vote counts for little, and surveys show that they grossly underestimate the costs of government activities, and so underestimate their significance, often leading to very low turnouts at elections. This problem is one reason why many Public Choice scholars, particularly those in the Virginia School, are so absorbed by the question of how governments might be restrained by constitutional and structural reforms.

The political income of politicians

As we have seen, one of the key insights of Public Choice, dating back to Black and Downs, is that the 'vote motive' is key to the positions that politicians and political parties take on policy issues. Opposition politicians may have some influence on events, but to have any real impact, they need to be in power. And to be in power, they need to be elected. In other words, they have a crucial interest in getting votes. They may seek power so that they can benefit humanity, rather than for any venal reason, but even so, their key objective must be to gather votes.

To garner votes, politicians have to be what the Chicago School describe as 'brokers' between competing interests – between, for example, the lobby groups that demand legislation and the taxpayers and consumers who ultimately pay for it. The 'brokerage fees' they pull in are votes; but if they are successful in that, they can enjoy many other kinds of 'political income' too. There may be generous campaign contributions; the status and perks of office; the deference of civil servants and the public; the public attention that comes from supporting popular causes; and the power to steer spending and employment to one's own district.

There may be cash implications too. With status comes the prospect of lucrative careers after politics. There may even be kickbacks, in terms of cash or favours, from lobbyists or government contractors. But it is a moot point whether selling a policy in a corrupt deal for cash is any different to, or any worse than, selling it for votes in a logrolling situation.

The dangers of the vote motive

One might think that the vote motive of politicians is little different from the profit motive of entrepreneurs in the market. One aims to collect money by giving the public what they want, the other aims to collect votes. But again, we must remember that market choices are voluntary, while political choices require an element of coercion. And the votes that politicians seek to collect might well not reflect the opinions and preferences of the wider public.

For example, the scale of the 'fees' paid to politicians will depend to some extent on how durable their 'customers' think their decisions and their time in office will turn out to be. But the best-paying customers will be small groups with concentrated interests, rather than the uninformed and diffused mass of the public. For that reason, politicians focus on the demands of well-organised, loud interest groups, and often give in to them – perhaps calculating that they can persuade the apathetic and uninformed public to go along with the decision.

The vote motive brings other problems too. For instance, politicians have a powerful incentive to support government spending in their own district, even if they know that it represents bad value for the country as a whole. Logrolling, in which they support equally bad projects in colleagues' districts, may spread that poor value even more widely. And omnibus legislation, designed to garner votes from many different groups, may have the same wasteful effect.

Another problem is the electoral bribery that goes on before elections, with politicians bidding for votes by supporting various popular causes – without necessarily explaining where the money to pay for them will come from. Only after the election is it explained that taxes have to rise. And it seems that political parties become slightly more centrist at elections as they try to pick up more of the voters bunched around the median, giving the public less of a real choice.

Public expenditure is easy to focus on particular groups, which in turn makes it easy to bid for their votes. Favouring such groups becomes all the easier when the government is large and has more power and money at its disposal. But the larger this network of favours grows, the less likely is it to reflect the interests of the wider public. And the larger, more complex and more powerful the state becomes, the greater is the scope for bribes and kickbacks.

Restraining our leaders

There remains, of course, the restraint of elections, by which the public can control their politicians, at least weakly. And the media might expose outright corruption. In addition, the fear of losing office may be enough to prevent governments being completely carefree with power and money – after all, if the opposition were elected, that same power and money could be used against them.

These restraints remain weak, however, and many Public Choice scholars, particularly those in the Virginia School, see constitutional rules as the best way of restraining our legislators. If the institutional rules favour incumbents, for example, politicians may be more likely to abuse their power than if they cannot expect a long term in office. Term limits and open primaries to select candidates for the legislature may reduce the power and patronage of the political parties. The US system of separation of powers makes it a little harder for logrolling and for deals with special interest groups to stick, since they might be overturned by another branch of government. But equally, in the USA the role of legislative committees, with their ability to thrash out logrolling trades, works in the opposite direction.

In the USA, the president has significant power, including the power of veto over congressional proposals. This again increases the chance of logrolling trades and special interest measures being unwound – when the proposal is sent back to Congress, a higher majority is required, making it harder for small minorities to push through their sectional interests. That makes lobbying riskier and less effective. It also allows the president to assert the wider national interest over legislation that might favour small minorities, such as people in a particular geographical region, over general consumers and taxpayers. Equally, however, strong and activist presidents can use their skill and power to break through the constitutional restraints and set up logrolling initiatives of their own.

The judiciary, similarly, may restrain politicians and prevent them from acting outside the law – or indeed outside the generally accepted rules of justice, even if the law passed in the legislature contradicts those deeper notions. Lifetime appointments, and non-political ways of choosing judges, may each give the judiciary greater independence from legislators and make judges more inclined to contradict the legislature, which again reduces the brokering power of government politicians. But where judicial appointments are made within a political process, it is more likely that judges will be political, or that 'stealth' candidates (who appear independent but are not) will be appointed, or that centrist candidates who attract the support of both sides will be appointed over genuinely independent outsiders.

In any event, there are limits to the extent to which judges can simply strike down the law of the land. Their principal function is to uphold it. And by doing that, they may find themselves simply enforcing the legislative bargains that have been brokered by politicians whose personal interests may not reflect those of the wider public.

9 MOTIVATING BUREAUCRATS

Another important part of the political process is the bureaucracy – the civil servants and other public officials who work in ministries, agencies, public bodies and local government. They are all needed to translate the decisions of legislators into practical action, and to apply broad policies appropriately to individual cases. But again, how far can we rely on them to do that dispassionately, rather than to let their own personal interests intervene?

Not much, according to many Public Choice scholars. Gordon Tullock, himself a former Foreign Office civil servant, wrote an early paper on his experiences in the bureaucracy. It much influenced James Buchanan, who formulated a theory that government bureaucrats had a strong interest in expanding the size and scope of the government sector. Another Virginia School author, William A. Niskanen, took up the theme, suggesting that a large motivator for public servants was the size of their own budgets, since that brought with it many other personal benefits.

This is in stark contrast to the approach of traditional welfare economists, in which officials were simply assumed to be objective and public-spirited, impartially pursuing the intent of the legislation they are charged to administer. In the Public Choice view, rational choice applies as much to bureaucrats as anyone else: within the limits of their powers and institutional structure, they try to maximise their personal ambitions. They may well seek to do a good job and to serve the public diligently; but like the rest of us, they also seek income, wealth, ease, tenure, seniority, leisure and comfort; and in their case, perhaps discretionary power and deference too.

In the bureaucracy, there is extensive scope for such self-serving action, partly because the output of public officials can be hard to define. Unlike market production, where success is measured in financial profit or loss, the officials' performance is hard to monitor, being based on objectives that are often vague – such as the ill-defined 'public interest'. So it should be no surprise if bureaucrats make time to pursue their own objectives too. Indeed, there is a much-discussed principal–agent problem within private businesses. Ultimately, there are mechanisms for the principals (shareholders) to hold the agents (management) to account – through selling shares, takeovers, appointing new boards, developing new forms of corporate governance, and through competition in the marketplace from better-run firms. Those mechanisms do not work perfectly but they are far more effective than the mechanisms by which principals (electors) are able to hold agents (bureaucrats) to account via a quinquennial election and the actions of political representatives.

Officials and budgets

In terms of what bureaucrats actually do pursue, Niskanen suggested that *budget maximisation* provided a fair measure. It is an approximation to the objective of profit in the market context. And it provides a simple proxy for all the other things that go with a large and growing budget – such as job security, promotion prospects, salary increases and so on.

In their pursuit of these benefits, bureaucrats are just as much players in the political process as any other interest group – and they have no free-rider problem because their group is so well defined that they can easily keep the benefits of their lobbying to themselves.

They do, of course, rely on the support of politicians for their budgets. But, however the budget is settled, says Niskanen, they are able to maximise their own benefit within it. If budget conditions are easy, they can simply take on new functions and demand more money to deal with the increased output. In tight conditions, they can limit their output and ensure that money sticks with them rather than being spent on projects.

Either way, says Niskanen, they manage to expand themselves beyond the size and scale that a median voter or politician would ever want. Bureaucrats have no personal interest in saving money, and every incentive to invent new work-streams and social programmes. And the bureaucrats know that it is hard for politicians to backtrack on a policy they have committed to, even if the bureaucratic cost escalates well beyond their original expectations. This again gives the bureaucracy considerable bargaining power over the legislature.

Bureaucrats can also resist budget reductions by threatening to cut important front-line services: Gordon Tullock cited the Federal Customs Service, which responded to budget cuts by laying off every front-line customs inspector in the USA, but none in any other part of the service.

The sources of bureaucratic power

The fact that legislation is generally rather vague gives the bureaucracy a great deal of discretionary power. Some Public Choice scholars suggest that politicians like it that way: they prefer to pass vague laws and set up self-preserving agencies to administer them, rather than pass detailed laws that their political opponents could simply overturn should they come into office. Whatever the reason, this large area of uncertainty in the law gives bureaucrats plenty of scope to define their own output and then demand budgets to match.

According to Niskanen, business people are exposed to the scrutiny of well-informed customers and analysts, but bureaucrats are not. The fact that bureaucrats are far more knowledgeable about their own particular area than the average politician means that politicians cannot effectively control the bureaucracy. And this monopoly of inside knowledge about their own function enables them to use the 'bundling' strategy to protect their empires: by being opaque about which parts of their function could be scaled back or prised off, they present politicians with a single package which the politicians have to take or leave.

Bureaucrats are also likely to design, promote and support complex policy initiatives that both increase their scope for discretion and help them to conceal how their budget is spent, so adding to the bewilderment of the politicians who are supposed to be controlling them.

Since they work so closely with politicians, there is even the unspoken threat that bureaucrats could humble their political masters by leaking damaging information about them, a threat that again might help them to resist attempts to cut their budgets. And the larger that government becomes, and the more decisions that politicians have to make, the greater is the chance that they will make bad decisions that could later be used to embarrass them.

Bureaucrats can also rely on the political support of the interest groups that depend on the grants and programmes that they administer, and which would almost certainly like to see those budgets increased; and they can rely on the support of the commercial businesses that supply goods and services to the programmes that the agencies administer. Another potential source of bureaucratic power is the voting power of the bureaucrats themselves. If the government employs a quarter or a third of the workforce, as it now does in many countries, public servants and their dependants form a huge voting bloc that is generally likely to favour more government bureaucracy and bigger bureaucratic budgets.

Restraining the bureaucracy

What techniques might help bring bureaucratic interests into line with those of the public, or even with those of politicians? One idea might be to introduce some measure of competition between different agencies. They might be forced to bid against the private sector for the supply of their services – a technique common in functions such as rubbish collection and highway maintenance. Or a large agency might be split into regional agencies, which allows their performance to be compared – as often happens in policing, for example.

Agencies could, perhaps, be paid only by the results they achieve, rather than by means of block grants that they use at their discretion. But this means trying to put a price on outputs that are difficult to define, never mind measure. Even the idea of making agencies compete against private providers is problematic: it requires some other public agency to review and award the contracts, and the weight of experience is that public agencies are not very good at such procurement.

More recent questions

Niskanen's rather gloomy view of bureaucracy, however, has been subjected to new techniques such as game theory, and to more recent questioning.

Some modern Public Choice scholars argue that politicians do, in fact, have considerable power to control bureaucrats. They can punish them through budget cuts and professional sanctions. They can harass them with enquiries. They can threaten public exposure and humiliation if bureaucratic incompetence or impropriety comes to light: simply punishing a few may be enough to keep others in line. They can threaten legislation to curb agencies that stray outside their legitimate brief. They can also build incentives into new legislation, with the aim of raising standards and performance and preventing bureaucratic excesses.

So managing the bureaucracy may not need detailed control. Even so, politicians may be better at detailed control of the bureaucracy than Niskanen and others first thought. Agencies tend to be regulated not by the legislature as a whole, but by specialist committees. The legislators who sit on those committees are likely to be just as expert in the government functions they manage as are the bureaucrats whom they oversee. That again might be quite enough to provide adequate control.

And yet, practical attempts to rein back a growing bureaucracy have come to grief in many countries. It is much easier for politicians to create new agencies than to abolish or curb them. And there is more political advantage in expanding than in cutting. A burgeoning bureaucracy, one might argue, is merely a symptom of things that are more fundamentally wrong in the way our democratic system works. And what we need to cure those ills, many Public Choice scholars insist, is much better constitutional controls.

10 THE ROLE OF CONSTITUTIONS

The logic of Public Choice does not doom us inevitably to being exploited by interest groups, our legislators or the bureaucracy. The Virginia School branch of the Public Choice approach gives particular emphasis to the role of constitutions as a means by which people can protect themselves against such abuse. And it explores the kind of constitution that rational self-interested individuals would create in order to do so.

In *The Calculus of Consent*, Buchanan and Tullock start by explaining why we need government in the first place. Anarchy, they say, is an undesirable state. Weak individuals would find themselves being abused by the strong, while even the strong would prefer a productive peace to the constant, destructive threat of hostility from others. In these circumstances, the institution of the state simply evolves as people forge a series of one-to-one agreements between each other in their attempt to escape from the anarchy.

By agreeing to mutual self-restraint, individuals can reduce their exposure to predation by others; by agreeing to contribute to mutual protection, they can spare themselves some of the high cost of self-protection; and by agreeing to collective action, they can undertake constructive projects that would be too large to do on their own.

But it does not require some physical assembly of everyone

to thrash out this system of agreement. Buchanan and Tullock see it as the outcome of countless numbers of one-to-one agreements between individuals. That network of agreements expands to form an unplanned system – much as countless numbers of civil court judgements grow to form the system of the common law, or countless bilateral trades form a market. It may look as if it is shaped by some conscious overall design, but in fact this social order just emerges and grows naturally out of the actions of rational and self-interested individuals.

The costs of decision-making

Nor is anyone forced into this network of agreements. Buchanan and Tullock saw people's acceptance of it as entirely voluntary. In order to be part of the general social agreement and share its benefits, individuals might have to accept some curbs on their own behaviour, but they will regard that as preferable to being in a state of anarchy. So agreement will be completely unanimous: nobody can be forced into an agreement that they think might leave them worse off, just as nobody in a free market can be forced to accept an unfavourable bargain.

The problems start, however, when it comes to deciding exactly what collective actions will be undertaken. While such action could indeed promote mutual protection, it could also be used to exploit minorities. There is no chance of such exploitation if the collective decisions have to be unanimous, since anyone who felt threatened by any policy would simply veto it. But unanimity means high *decision-making costs*: it may prove very difficult to reach agreement on almost anything if a single individual can block every proposal. The *external costs* of potential exploitation may be avoided, but a unanimity rule could mean that we also miss out on many of the potential gains from collective action because we can never agree. Conversely, of course, a rule that requires something less than unanimity might make it easier to take decisions, but leaves individuals with the risk that they could be exploited.

Buchanan and Tullock say that the way out of this conundrum is to have a two-stage process. The first stage is the *constitutional* stage, in which people agree on the areas that need collective decision-making, and which sets the *rules* by which future decisions are to be taken. Only when the agenda and the decision-making rules are decided do we move on to the second stage, of actually making collective decisions on what to do. The constitutional stage is about *what* should be decided on, and *how*; after that our attention turns to actually making choices. For example, say Buchanan and Tullock, oil drillers may agree that there should be collective management of an oilfield, and on how decisions on extraction rights might be made; but at the second stage, they might well disagree on the specific quotas that are assigned them when those decisions are actually taken.

The constitutional agreement, say Buchanan and Tullock, is necessarily unanimous: no rational and self-interested person would agree to adopt a set of decision-making rules that they thought would give rise to future decisions that would exploit them. Such unanimity might seem a tall order, but in general people will be keen to reach agreement in order to enjoy the protection of society and escape the state of anarchy; and since nobody knows precisely how the future decisions will affect them, everyone is likely to insist on the same sorts of checks and protections.

The content of a constitution

One thing a constitution will have to settle is the majority that is used to make subsequent collective decisions.

There is a natural tendency among people to assume that a simple majority is the right rule for group choices. After all, going with the majority is what we do in most of the everyday decisions we make among friends and colleagues. But there are many possible voting rules and there is nothing special about simple majority voting. Indeed, a company, when forming its constitution, will have different voting rules for different types of decisions. Members' clubs have a similar procedure. A group of 51 per cent of the population would not seem to have much greater legitimate authority than a group of 49 per cent; yet in majority votes, that first group gets to dominate the second.

Buchanan and Tullock suggest that it might make sense to insist on larger, or 'qualified', majorities for some votes, particularly where there is a high risk that minority groups would be exploited, and where the potential size of that exploitation could be severe. Indeed, they believe that rational individuals would insist on such constitutional safeguards. At the constitutional stage, individuals face future *uncertainty*: they do not know what future policy proposals will come up, and whether they will be on the winning or the losing side; so individuals will want to protect themselves against the possibility of suffering major losses at the hands of the majority. Individuals might accept that a requirement of unanimity in every vote would be far too cumbersome; but some qualified majority, say a two-thirds rule, might make sense for some potentially very damaging decisions.

A constitution drawn up by self-interested individuals will also place limits on the powers given to legislators. While it makes sense to appoint representatives to take decisions, rather than for the whole public to have to struggle with the detail of every proposal, it would be very dangerous to give elected officials complete decision-making power. Not only would that mean that individuals and minorities could suffer serious damage as a result of the legislature's decisions; we also know from experience that power corrupts, and that representatives cannot be trusted with too much of it. So a constitution should limit what legislators, and indeed bureaucrats, can decide.

Buchanan's fiscal constitution

According to Buchanan, there is a need for especially careful controls on tax policy, since this is a field in which majority decisions can cause particularly severe damage to minority groups. The tax rules, therefore, should be defined and stated at the outset – and rational individuals will make sure that they are. One might imagine, for example, that poorer people might vote for a tax code that puts heavy burdens on the rich; but constitutions are meant to last – renegotiating them all the time would be far too exacting – and given a reasonable measure of social mobility, nobody quite knows where they might end up in a number of years' time. You may be in the majority group now, but that will not necessarily last. The rational choice, for rich and poor alike, is to support a tax system that treats all groups equally.

It is the same with spending. Buchanan believes that only spending for general benefit would be agreed unanimously at the constitutional stage. It is pointless to try to skew the rules to favour your own particular group when you may no longer be in that group in a few years' time. This is, Buchanan admits, very far from where we are at the moment, since so much state spending has been captured by special interest groups for their own benefit. It would be difficult to get from here to the kind of non-discriminatory constitution that he believes rational individuals should favour; perhaps some of these groups, such as welfare beneficiaries, would have to be bought off before we could put non-discriminatory constitutional rules in place.

Buchanan believes that sound constitutional tax rules would limit the total tax burden, and ensure that the base on which tax is levied cannot be manipulated to benefit particular interests. Indeed, there would have to be rules on how far the burden of taxation and the benefits of public spending could be shifted between different groups. There would need to be a balanced budget, so that majorities could not simply time-shift, voting themselves benefits today and leaving future generations to pay for them. Taxes would have to be earmarked for the purpose for which they were levied. There would have to be solid rules on property ownership and how far the state could eat into private property. And there would need to be rules on the government's production of money so that the currency could not be debased – a kind of stealth tax on the public, and one which harms some groups (such as savers) much more than others (such as debtors).

Without unanimous rules of this sort, argues Buchanan, there is a constant risk that the state will over-expand, favouring some groups, putting the burden on others and generally undermining incentives.

Federalism

Another way to limit power is to divide it, and the Virginia School is keen on such localism and federalism. There is a trade-off between the costs and benefits of making decisions centrally and locally. It is easier to reach decisions in small groups than in large ones, so it makes sense to take decisions as locally as possible. National governments may look impressive, but the very size of their electorates makes it harder to reach agreement.

There is another factor too: the homogeneity of the population. It will be much easier to reach agreement if the electorate shares common aims, values and approaches, than in a population that has more diverse views and opinions.

If a population is extremely large and extremely heterogeneous, it might not be possible to reach collective decisions on many things at all. In this case, choices are best left to private action rather than public – and probably will be. The USA might be an example of such a large and diverse society. If, however, a population is small and homogeneous, agreement will be easier and we should expect more decisions to be made collectively – as is generally true, for example, in the small and homogeneous societies of Scandinavia.

Certainly, there are some decisions that can only be made at the national level: national economic policy, for example, or the provision of a national defence network. There are also policies that might be good for one geographical area but cause problems for another – such as when a new industrial development pollutes the water that flows downriver through other cities.

Generally, though, political choices are best made as locally as possible. Some decisions, after all – whether to license a new nightclub, for instance – have a purely local impact, so it is pointless trying to get general agreement on them at the national level. Federal systems also allow government structures, services, laws and regulations to be tailored to suit the specific needs of the locality.

Another advantage of localism is that it becomes possible to escape if you do not like what is decided. If the local majority threaten to exploit you, you can simply move somewhere else. That may not be pleasant or easy, especially if you have deep roots in your home locality; but the fact that it is possible imposes a limit on the ability of local authorities to exploit minorities.

Problems and principles

The Virginia School's constitutional outlook does not convince everyone. Many critics argue that people are not as risk-averse as Buchanan and Tullock paint them, and that they might well regard the enormous potential benefits of collective decisions as being well worth the risk of having to pay higher taxes.

And the fact is that we have constitutions and conventions that were not chosen by the unanimous consent of everyone. People today find themselves bound by old constitutional rules drawn up by their forebears, in which they have had no say at all. Many of the world's constitutions were drawn up by narrow majorities, or have been hijacked by interest groups, or can be amended by simple majorities in the legislature. Majority decisions in Britain's parliament, for example, have changed the powers and membership of the House of Lords, and ceded many functions to European Union institutions, without seeking any permission from the British public, unanimous or otherwise. And Parliament is sovereign: there are no constitutional restraints on its power to tax or to confiscate property. Yet the fact that most people choose not to emigrate cannot be taken as evidence that they tacitly agree to this 'constitution'.

Nevertheless, the Virginia School's constitutional theory brought decisive change to economic and political theory. Economists once thought they knew how to design bold policy initiatives that would raise the overall welfare of society. But the Virginia School pointed out that economists cannot see into the hearts and minds of individuals, and know how they value such policy changes. The only way is to ask them whether they feel better off; but even then, we cannot compare one person's loss with another's gain. It is only if there is complete agreement that we can say for sure that the new arrangement is beneficial. And when we are looking at a durable constitution that decides how future policies are decided, that is a particularly important thing to get right.

11 ACHIEVEMENTS AND ISSUES

Public Choice has made a big difference to how economists, political scientists and perhaps even the public view the workings of the political process. It explains how the mechanics of our political institutions, and the personal interests of those involved, shape the decisions that are made in the name of the public. Questions remain about how far some parts of the approach fit the real world, especially when so many different political systems abound; but perhaps this just shows that Public Choice is a young discipline, with a great deal of potential ahead of it.

Some achievements

Public Choice has certainly succeeded in challenging economists' unthinking assumption that government intervention is a perfect solution to 'market failure'. It reminds us that there is 'government failure' too; and that shortcomings such as monopolies, imperfect information and the fact that some actions have adverse effects on bystanders are more common in politics than in markets. The very process of government decision-making is itself imperfect, being distorted by the oddities of electoral systems, tactical voting, the power of interest-group coalitions and the personal interests of legislators and officials. In many cases, we might well be better simply to accept the market reality and not to use the apparatus of the state to intervene at all.

Public Choice has also undermined economists' assumption that the 'public interest' is something that can be identified by experts and achieved through enlightened policy. On the contrary: there are as many opinions on the 'public interest' as there are individuals, and the views and values of those individuals are personal to themselves and cannot be added, subtracted and averaged through some arithmetical formula.

Another achievement of Public Choice has been to focus attention on the actual workings of government, and to make us question how well we are served by our current political institutions. It clarifies the nature, origins and wider political effects of such phenomena as interest groups, coalitions, logrolling, rent seeking, the growth of government, tactical voting and the rational ignorance of electors. Its focus on the personal interests of voters, legislators and officials helps explain why the public are so sceptical about politics. It shows us how the nature of the political institutions we live under makes a critical difference to what collective choices are made. It demonstrates how political institutions so often fail. And it reminds us that there are alternatives, such as qualified majority voting and alternative vote or transferable vote systems, and constitutional reforms, which may help reduce government failure.

A question of self-interest

Nevertheless, other parts of the Public Choice approach remain controversial. Some people, for example, question whether the rational individualism that underpins it is actually a good description of human personality. After all, we are social animals, and our animal and social context shapes what we do and what we think. There is a large genetic element to our personality, over which we may have limited rational control. We work in groups – indeed, many people criticise the financial sector for its 'herd mentality' in following investment trends. Many, perhaps most, of the choices we make are instinctive, or the natural outcome of years of social pressure, rather than the product of rational calculation. Are we really as rational, and as individualist, as Public Choice scholars imagine?

Or again: is politics even about rational individuals making exchanges aimed at benefiting themselves? Is it in fact about power, whereby different individuals and groups try to force others into complying with their wishes? Public Choice scholars say it is the first – or at least that the second is a consequence of the first – but focus much of their attention on the second, exploring the power of majorities and of concentrated interest groups.

The question of why supposedly rational individuals bother to vote at all remains a pertinent question here, since any single vote is extremely unlikely to decide an election – and even if it did, the consequences of that for the individual voter are extremely uncertain. Do we perhaps need some deeper explanation than the economic approach can give us, something based within human social psychology?

In response, Public Choice scholars would argue that it does not matter exactly how and from where people's motives originate. The important thing is that we do have values and motives and desires and that we seek to maximise them, whatever they are. We may want to be part of the crowd; or we may aspire to help our fellow human beings, or to live honourably, or have countless other noble ambitions. By pursuing those aims, we are in fact serving our own desires – our own interests. We may well make ourselves financially poorer by giving charity to those who need it; but we still count ourselves as better off for having done it. Public Choice scholars also argue that it is prudent to assume that self-interest will be a motivating factor within the political system – not that it motivates all people at all times in all situations.

Constitutional issues

Other questions remain too. If politicians (and for that matter voters) really are self-interested, will any set of constitutional rules contain them and bring their interests into line with those of the public? Buchanan argues that there is a great deal right with the US constitution – such as its division of power between two legislative houses, a president and the judiciary, and the legislature's qualified majority voting on presidential vetoes and constitutional amendments. Even so, US politics remains rife with logrolling and rent seeking, and the role and powers of legislators and officials continue to expand. This is, in Buchanan's own words, more of a 'constitutional anarchy' than a restrained government.

Some critics have more general concerns about the Virginia School's focus on constitutions. Even the US constitution is not a matter of unanimous agreement. Can we really suggest that people who have never voted on it somehow tacitly consent to it? The sad truth is that populations will put up with various political injustices for a surprisingly long time. The social pressure to conform, and perhaps the force of authority, remains strong. A revolution might be needed to escape the constitutional anarchy, but the existing elites certainly have no interest in driving it; and the diffused interests of the general public mean there may be no sparking point for reform.

And would people, trying to escape from the state of anarchy, actually be as worried about giving power to governments as the Virginia School constitutional theorists suggest? Might people in fact be willing to take the risk that they might be exploited at some future time, in order to give themselves the large and obvious benefits of collective action?

These are questions that experimental economics is now helping to solve. For instance, there is a famous theory by John Rawls that if people had to choose a social arrangement without knowing what their place in it would be, they would choose one with a high minimum income rather than take the risk of living in abject poverty. But experiments by Norman Frohlich and others in 1987 showed that students never choose this arrangement: they are far more likely to prefer a society in which average incomes are maximised – albeit with some floor, but quite a low floor. In other words, they are willing to take at least some risk concerning their own future. So, contrary to Buchanan and Tullock, might people not be willing to take risks in constitutional settlements too?

Self-interested Public Choice?

Another criticism that has been made of Public Choice advocates is that they too bring their own self-interest to the discipline. Many Public Choice scholars – James M. Buchanan, William A. Niskanen and Gordon Tullock of the Virginia School, and Gary S. Becker and George J. Stigler of Chicago, to name just a few – would count themselves as liberals (in the European, rather than the American, sense). So are the restraints they propose on government just a symptom of their dislike of state power?

Their reply would be simple. Public Choice scholars are well aware that markets are not perfect; but Public Choice reveals that government action suffers from fundamental shortcomings too. It is quite easy to demonstrate that the ultimate effect of majority voting, and the presence of interest groups, rent seeking and all the rest, is to create a government sector that is inefficiently large. That is not a political statement, but a matter of practical and economic fact. Their aim, they would say, is only to explain this; and in some cases, to propose institutional changes that might help to correct it.

The Chicago School, in particular, focuses more on the pure economics of government. It analyses Public Choice issues in terms of pure microeconomic theory – applying the tools of neoclassical price theory, equilibrium analysis and rational choice. It avoids making value judgements about the nature of public decision-making processes, viewing government instead as a 'political market', through which rational, self-interested 'economic' agents pursue their own interests and seek to redistribute wealth across the community. It sees policy decisions, for example, as the 'price' that balances the supply of government laws and regulations with the 'demand' for them from the public. It asks how well these political markets work, and to what extent they are technically efficient. If people want to protect agricultural jobs, for example, are farm subsidies an efficient way to do it? How well do interest groups succeed in steering community resources towards themselves?

This application of pure microeconomics to Public Choice questions has taken Chicago scholars, such as Gary Becker, into applying the same analysis to related policy issues such as the economics of crime, education, the family, immigration and altruism, with interesting and sometimes surprising results.

In general, the conclusions of the Chicago School are not usually far from those of the Virginia School, though it may be harder to lay the charge of self-interest against the leaders of the Chicago School, rejecting ideology and attempting to be coldly scientific as it does. If there is a criticism to be made of Chicago, however, it might be that many of the school's assumptions – that coalition-building is easy, that free-riding can be restrained or that interest groups work efficiently – are too rarefied. They are – deliberately – like the 'perfect competition' assumptions in economics: we know this perfect world can never exist, but working out its principles nevertheless provides us with some interesting and useful insights. The problem comes when people confuse the abstract theory with the reality. For example, while scientific economists may regard buying votes and buying off people in the marketplace as little different and equally efficient in economic terms, the general public would find the suggestion of open bribery for votes deeply shocking.

12 CURRENT AND FUTURE HORIZONS

The 'second generation' of Public Choice scholars subjected the 'first-generation' ideas of Duncan Black, Anthony Downs, Mancur Olson, James M. Buchanan, Gordon Tullock and William H. Riker to deeper scrutiny, testing them against a wider array of assumptions and political systems. One line of research was to examine more closely how the individual opinions of voters could best be 'aggregated' into some collective decision that would truly reflect those individual views.

In particular, attention focused on how to make the process 'strategy-proof' – in other words, how to prevent groups of voters from manipulating the outcome by lying about their true preferences and voting tactically rather than sincerely. That is important both to democrats, to whom the thought of such manipulation by vested interests is distasteful, and to political scientists and politicians, who cannot know whether a collective choice actually reflects voters' opinions unless voters actually express their opinions honestly.

A theorem by Allan Gibbard and Mark Satterthwaite, however, suggested that democratic elections were always open to strategic voting. And there is still the problem that one-person-one-vote systems, as in the two wolves and one sheep case, do not reveal the strength of feeling of the individual voters. So attention turned instead to what kind of a system might reveal people's true preferences – what Public Choice scholars call *demand revelation*.

Edward H. Clarke and Theodore Groves argued that one way to reveal the true strength of people's desires would be to charge them an 'incentive tax' equal to the costs that their decisions imposed on others. This would force the wolves to take into account the effect of their decisions on the sheep. Dennis C. Mueller devised a three-step voting procedure to expose people's real preferences. And various other mathematical and practical suggestions have been proposed and tested, such as having several rounds of elections in the style of French or US presidential elections. Such research exposes other interesting questions too: such as how far voters are rational, and whether they adapt to past electoral experience, or whether they are indeed largely uninformed and myopic.

On the other hand, Public Choice work in the 1980s suggested that the two-party system that the first-generation scholars focused on actually produces collective decisions that reflect voters' preferences rather better than had been supposed. This is because, like competition in the marketplace, competition between parties leads them to modify their own positions and produce policy platforms that in fact are attractive to large sections of the public.

Nevertheless, many of the world's political systems are multi-party systems in which forming a government depends on putting together a coalition of different parties. So 'second-generation' attention, led by the Rochester School, focused more on how parties form coalitions and on how long those coalitions were likely to endure. This is what led to William H. Riker's idea of the *minimum winning coalition*, and subsequently to the proposition that large central parties, being essential to any coalition, can and often do choose to form minority governments and rely on issue-by-issue voting pacts rather than formal partnerships.

More recently, in his book *Perfecting Parliament*, Roger Congleton traces the history of legislatures in six major countries, explaining the importance of self-interest, social ideas, religion and the existing state of institutions, authority and relationships in determining the development of electoral and legislative rules. Plainly, most countries are quite far from the rational sort of constitutional arrangements proposed by Buchanan and Tullock.

Reconsideration of old ideas

In addition to taking Public Choice into new areas such as multi-party systems, the second generation has started to test some of the founding concepts of the discipline, sometimes to near-destruction.

Practical investigations have raised doubts about the median voter principle, for example. It seems that parties do tend to be slightly more centrist in their positioning just before elections. But parties do not simply rush to support anything they believe might appeal to centrist voters. After all, they may have years of ideology and history behind them, not to mention an established body of policy to maintain. Their own activists will resist any dilution of that agenda, which they helped create; and the electorate too may well reject a lurch to the centre as unprincipled opportunism.

The simple theory of the median voter also loses some of its value in the context of multi-party politics, complex and interrelated issues, bicameral legislatures and large and diverse electorates. As Public Choice applies itself to a widening array of political systems, the simple theory again loses its central relevance.

Another idea that has been reconsidered is the 'free-rider' problem that is used to justify the compulsory provision of public goods. Recent research in Public Choice has suggested that, while people do indeed free-ride, they do so much less than might be supposed. Perhaps human beings are more public-spirited, social and cooperative creatures than we give them credit for. But equally, this may be yet another challenge to the strict individualism and self-interest that formed the very foundation of Public Choice thinking.

Second-generation debates

The second generation of Public Choice thinkers included figures such as William A. Niskanen and George J. Stigler. Another is Dennis C. Mueller, who investigated how high-ranking politicians and officials use their inside knowledge to advance their own agendas and enlarge their empires at the expense of the public – pointing out that corporate managers do much the same, at the expense of their shareholders. The pessimism that these authors shared with the first generation has been questioned, however, by some later scholars.

For example, Niskanen's view that it was impossible for legislators to control bureaucrats has been questioned: legislative committees have sometimes proved to be very well informed about their agencies, suggesting that broad controls may be enough to contain the bureaucracy.

Stigler's equally pessimistic view – that regulatory agencies are not just captured by well-organised special interest groups, but are, in fact, largely set up for their benefit – has also come under fire in recent years. Stigler's 'third-generation' Chicago colleague Gary S.

Becker argued that large, diffuse groups actually have a lot more voting power than Stigler (and perhaps Olson) supposed. Meanwhile, the Chicago-trained economist James Q. Wilson suggested that the combination of concentrated benefits and diffused costs that makes regulatory institutions ripe for capture is, in fact, just one special case, since several other combinations are theoretically possible. (While this is theoretically true, however, it remains the institutional capture case that most troubles democrats.)

Vincent Ostrom, another second-generation thinker, sought a way out of the prevailing Public Choice pessimism by looking at how collective decision-making might be improved by splitting up the process between different centres. This is akin to competition in the market sector, which is generally reckoned to produce better results than monopoly provision. Ostrom argues that 'polycentric' decision-making improves the quality and stability of collective choices, and is better tuned to the inherent diversity of the population.

Third-generation frontiers

Gary S. Becker and colleagues at the Chicago School have attempted to go deeper into the pure theory of the economics of politics. They see politics as a 'market' in which different political demands are balanced, just as demands for goods and services are balanced in commercial markets.

Virginia School scholars such as Charles K. Rowley, however – prominent for his work on the importance of limited government – criticise this as an abstract view that defends many institutions (such as US tort law and long-term trade barriers) as 'economically efficient' when they are in fact politically indefensible.

Others such as Bruno S. Frey argue that there is more to political life than mere economic factors – and that non-financial motives such as self-esteem are critically important. Indeed, Barry Weingast has almost reversed the Chicago approach, exploring how *political* considerations shape the nature of *commercial* markets.

Meanwhile, other third-generation scholars have taken Public Choice into interesting new avenues. Robert D. Tollison, for example, has shown how the rise of parliament in the late medieval age led to the decline in monopolies because it now required a majority in the legislature, not just the consent of the monarch, to create them. And there may be lessons in this for our institutions today.

Game theory

A particularly fruitful recent aspect of modern Public Choice is game theory, and in particular what is known as evolutionary game theory. Game theory explores what people do when their choices are critically dependent on the actions of others. The classic example is the *prisoner's dilemma*, in which two prisoners both confess because they fear harsher punishment if they remain silent and the other implicates them.

This sort of reasoning is very relevant in voting situations, particularly those in which people might try to anticipate how others will vote and then vote strategically, in order to improve the chances of their own favoured candidates or outcomes, or to prevent others from succeeding. By working out how people 'game' the choices before them, we may be able to design systems that will expose their real preferences and therefore produce a result that is more in tune with the public's real wishes and which cannot be so easily manipulated by organised interest groups.

There is also another fascinating use for this game theory. Peter Ordeshook – who trained at Rochester and was one of William H. Riker's co-authors – uses it to identify electoral fraud, focusing in particular on the new democracies of the former Soviet bloc.

Moving on from the pure theory of electoral gaming, economists have found it fruitful to conduct practical experiments on how real people do actually behave when faced with choices such as those they face in elections and politics. The Nobel laureate Vernon Smith, for instance, ran experiments to see how people's real preferences might be revealed when groups faced repeated – 'iterated' – choices rather than just one-off elections, allowing them to see how others actually behaved when asked to vote. He found that student volunteers did tend to reach compromises which made everyone better off without making some people worse off – the *Pareto optimality* that economists and political scientists dream of. This suggests that there may be some virtue in electoral systems that depend on repeated rounds of voting. The experiments also suggest that it is indeed possible to reach a unanimous choice in such situations, a finding from which the Virginia School constitutional theorists must take heart.

Future potential

The emergence and growth of diverse new democracies has given Public Choice a new importance as new nations look to its findings for lessons on how their own constitutional, legislative and electoral systems should be constructed. In the process, Public Choice has had to expand out of the traditional US and UK two-party majority-voting models that were familiar to its founders and deal with a much wider range of different systems.

Established democracies too have been taking lessons from Public Choice. There is more recognition of the private interests of legislators and bureaucrats, and of the need to restrain them. Such policies are becoming more common: sunset legislation to limit the lifetime of public agencies and programmes, privatisation and deregulation, tax simplification, competition between and within government agencies, market testing for public provision, constitutional caps on government borrowing and other measures.

As attention moves beyond the traditional US and UK systems, Public Choice scholars have gone more deeply into the workings of mechanisms such as proportional representation, multi-member seats and party list systems. There is also more exploration of the effects of different legislative structures, of different parliamentary rules, of the role of party or national leadership in setting the agenda and many other issues. The broad conclusion that the design of the political institutions is crucially important to the collective decisions that are made still remains; but at least now we know how universally true it is.

GLOSSARY

Agenda setter

Person such as the chair of a committee, who can exploit the Rock, Paper, Scissors *cycling* paradox by deciding the order in which votes are taken.

Chicago School

A branch of Public Choice pioneered by George J. Stigler and Gary Becker, which focuses on applying pure economic theory to the political 'market place'.

Cycling

Phenomenon noted by Condorcet, whereby, as in the game of Rock, Paper, Scissors, there is no clear winner that can defeat all others.

Demand revelation problem

The problem that most voting systems do not measure how intensely electors feel about the options on offer, and that some electors may vote tactically, rather than honestly. Thus the outcome of the voting process may not reflect electors' true beliefs and preferences.

Free-rider problem

The situation in which people cannot be excluded from enjoying the benefits of 'public' goods such as parks or national defence, and therefore do not contribute to their cost. This may lead to the under-provision or non-provision of such goods.

Game theory

Mathematical modelling of situations where an individual's choices depend on the actions of others used to attempt to predict the most likely outcomes.

Government failure

The situation whereby a government intervention may cause a less efficient allocation of resources than would have occurred without the intervention.

Impossibility theorem

Kenneth J. Arrow's conclusion that when voters have more than two options to choose from, no democratic voting system generates collective choices that truly reflect the nature, prevalence and strength of individual voters' preferences.

Logrolling

Vote trading for mutual benefit. There are two kinds: *explicit* logrolling, as in 'you vote for my measure and I will vote for yours'; and *implicit* logrolling, in which voters are faced with a package of measures that is pre-designed to pick up support from different groups.

Median voter theorem

Duncan Black's hypothesis that, on simple ('how much?') issues, political parties pitch their policy offerings around the centre of opinion, where most votes are to be had, leaving voters little real choice. Recent research, however, questions how strong this effect is.

Minimum winning coalition

William H. Riker's idea that, since large coalitions are hard to keep together, interest groups will seek to assemble a coalition that is just large enough to achieve their shared objectives.

Prisoners' dilemma

Hypothetical game theory case in which two captives both face lighter punishment if they confess and implicate the other, but harsher punishment if the other implicates them. Although both could escape punishment by remaining silent, the most likely outcome is that both confess and implicate the other.

Public good

A good such as a national park or defence, which many individuals can enjoy at once, and from which it is difficult to exclude people. These goods may be under-provided because of the *free-rider problem*.

Rational ignorance

Anthony Downs's point that since an individual vote is unlikely to turn an election, and that even then the policy that is adopted will have uncertain effects, it is not worth electors spending time and effort to become well informed about parties and policies.

Rational maximising

A central assumption in economics, that individuals attempt to maximise their personal satisfaction, and act purposively to that end. This does not imply that people are greedy or self-centred; their personal satisfaction may come in part from improving the lives of others such as friends, family or the wider public.

Rent seeking

Gordon Tullock's idea that favourable political decisions can deliver such great rewards to particular groups that it is worthwhile for interest groups to spend large amounts of time, money and effort on lobbying for them.

Rochester School

A branch of Public Choice pioneered by William H. Riker, which brought the techniques of statistical analysis, game theory and experimental economics to the study of political decision-making.

Strategic voting

The phenomenon by which electors vote for a candidate or option that does not reflect their true preference in order to prevent an even less desirable outcome.

Time shifting

Voting for benefits that are enjoyed today, such as higher state pensions or debt-funded new roads, but which will be paid for by future taxpayers.

Virginia School

A branch of Public Choice pioneered by James M. Buchanan and Gordon Tullock, which uses political theory to analyse real-world political institutions and make recommendations accordingly. A strong theme of this school is the importance of constitutional arrangements to prevent the exploitation of minorities.

Vote motive

Analogous to the 'profit motive' in the commercial marketplace, a phrase (from the title of a 1976 IEA paper by Gordon Tullock) to represent the driving force in the political marketplace.

PUBLIC CHOICE TIMELINE

1781 French nobleman Count Charles de Borda questions the effectiveness of simple majority rule and proposes a system whereby people instead rank candidates or options.

1785 The Marquis de Condorcet criticises Borda's proposal as being vulnerable to interest groups. He explains the 'paradox' whereby majority voting can produce inconsistent results. In his 'jury theorem', he also explains the wisdom of crowds.

1876 Mathematician Charles Dodgson (better known as the author Lewis Carroll) discovers the French ideas and proposes a complex voting system to end the Condorcet paradox and to produce consistent, favoured winners.

1896 Knut Wicksell's essay 'A new principle of just taxation' justifies collective action but argues that only unanimous voting can ensure a just distribution of tax and prevent minorities being exploited.

1948 Duncan Black rediscovers Borda's and Condorcet's ideas, makes them more widely available, and develops them. He outlines the 'median voter theorem', which implies that political parties are more likely to win elections by bidding for centrist voters. Black comes to be considered the founder of modern Public Choice economics.

1950 Kenneth Arrow shows that no practical and desirable voting procedure can overcome Condorcet's paradox.

1957 Anthony Downs applies economic ideas to voting, confirming Black's view that parties converge to the centre, highlighting the power of and rewards available to interest-group coalitions, and showing why voters remain 'rationally ignorant' of political issues.

1962 In *The Calculus of Consent*, James M. Buchanan and Gordon Tullock apply the idea of self-interest across the field of political science. They show how the difficulty of reaching unanimous agreement leads to the use of other systems such as majority rule and how these allow the majority to exploit the minority. To prevent this, they argue for unanimously agreed constitutional rules by which all other voting arrangements are governed. They also explore 'logrolling', by which interest groups vote for each other's measures, creating an excess of government.

1962 William H. Riker explains the importance of coalitions in elections, and why some succeed better than others – an early example of applying 'game theory' to the analysis of political processes.

1965 Mancur Olson applies economists' rational choice theory to politics, showing how relatively small interest groups can exert a significant effect on elections for their own benefit, while larger groups often find this difficult.

1965 Buchanan and Tullock create the Public Choice Society as a way to promote discussion on Public Choice theory. It flourishes and grows. Three of its presidents (Buchanan, Vernon Smith and Elinor Ostrom) go on to win the Nobel Prize in Economic Sciences.

1966 Tullock founds the journal that becomes *Public Choice*.

1967 Tullock argues that the huge potential value of politically derived monopolies makes interest groups campaign hard to get them – a behaviour subsequently named 'rent seeking' by Anne Krueger.

1971 William A. Niskanen argues that bureaucrats attempt to maximise the size of their budgets, and explores the implications of this in terms of decision-making and the size of government.

1971, Exploring the idea that people vote dishonestly for public benefits
1973 that others will be forced to pay for, Edward H. Clarke (1971) and Theodore Groves (1973) show how voters might be induced to reveal their true preferences by making them bear the costs that their choices impose on the minority. Other 'demand revelation' systems follow.

1979 Vernon L. Smith conducts experiments on voting systems and the feasibility of the unanimity rule. In 2002 he wins the Nobel Prize in Economic Sciences for his work in experimental economics.

1980s Various economic papers suggest that two-party systems are better at reflecting public preferences than some suppose – a sort of 'invisible hand' at work in politics.

1986 James Buchanan wins the Nobel Prize for his work on the constitutional bases of economic and political decision-making.

1987 Exploring what kind of a constitution might achieve general agreement, Norman Frohlich, Joe A. Oppenheimer and Cheryl L. Eavey find that students would vote for one that sets a social minimum but allows average incomes to be maximised – contra to John Rawls's conjecture that people would prefer a high minimum.

1990 Peter van Roozendaal explains how a centralist party can form a minority government by relying on others to left and right.

2000s Further experimentation and mathematical modelling on political choices, and expansion of Public Choice ideas into many countries.

2002 Vernon L. Smith wins the Nobel Prize in Economic Sciences for his experimental work, including that on collective choices.

2007 Bryan Caplan's *The Myth of the Rational Voter* argues that voters show irrational biases (make-work schemes, anti-foreign, pessimism, anti-market) that produce critical failures in the democratic process.

2009 Elinor Ostrom wins the Nobel Prize in Economic Sciences for work including the study of how groups make collective decisions over scarce resources.

FURTHER READING

Introductions

Rowley, Charles K. (2004), 'Public Choice from the perspective of the history of thought', in *The Encyclopaedia of Public Choice*, vol. 1. Excellent short history of the Public Choice approach and where it stands today.

Rowley, Charles K. and Friedrich Schneider (2008), *Readings in Public Choice and Constitutional Political Economy*. Relatively accessible multi-author outline of the relationship between constitutional theory and a range of political issues. Charles Rowley's essay 'Public Choice and constitutional political economy' provides a readable overview. Dennis Mueller's 'Public Choice: an introduction' is an excellent and readable history of the different generations of Public Choice thinking.

Tullock, Gordon (1976, 2006), *The Vote Motive*. Excellent, readable, widely translated and short book showing the relevance of Public Choice concepts to issues in voting, politics, bureaucracy and logrolling. http://www.iea.org.uk/sites/default/files/publications/files/upldbook397pdf.pdf

Tullock, Gordon, Arthur Seldon and Gordon Brady (2002), *Government Failure: A Primer in Public Choice*. Not really a primer, this book tackles a small number of issues such as rent seeking and logrolling, and reviews contemporary US and UK political issues from this perspective.

Overviews

Maclean, Iain (1987), *Public Choice: An Introduction*. Short book that outlines the basic Public Choice concepts such as the voter as a consumer, voting paradoxes, lobbying, coalitions and bureaucracy.

Mueller, Dennis C. (2003), *Public Choice III*. The comprehensive study of the discipline, but very detailed and really intended for academics, university students and experts.

Critiques

Glazer, Amihai and Lawrence Rothenberg (2005), *Why Government Succeeds and Why It Fails*. Uses the tools of Public Choice to provide a more positive view of government, though still mindful of the existence of government failure.

Hindmoor, Andrew (2006), *Rational Choice*. Excellent little book, critical of Public Choice from a political science perspective.

Classic texts

Arrow, Kenneth (1951, 1963), *Social Choice and Individual Values*. Explores how individuals' preferences shape social choices, and explains the 'impossibility' of finding a democratic arrangement that will achieve this perfectly.

Black, Duncan (1958), *The Theory of Committees and Elections*. Classic text outlining the science of politics, tracing its history back to Condorcet and Borda, and showing how different voting rules greatly affect the choices made.

Buchanan, James M. and Gordon Tullock (1962), *The Calculus of Consent*. Classic, though not easy, text that applies the individualist approach to constitution-building, and outlines the impact of logrolling and special interest groups on public choices. See also Buchanan's 1975 *The Limits of Liberty*, which outlines his theory of the contractarian basis and legitimate limits of the state.

Caplan, Bryan (2007), *The Myth of the Rational Voter*. A modern classic, which argues that most voters are subject to systematic biases, which (as the book's subtitle puts it) is 'Why democracies choose bad policies'.

Downs, Anthony (1957), *An Economic Theory of Democracy*. Outlines how the economic theory of rational self-interest can be applied to political decision-making and used to explain how collective choices are made.

Niskanen, William A. (1971), *Bureaucracy and Representative Government*; (1973), *Bureaucracy: Servant or Master?* IEA Hobart Paperback. These books extend the ideas of rational self-interest to public administrators, building a powerful critique of bureaucracy and its motives.

Olson, Mancur (1965), *The Logic of Collective Action*. Explores the nature of interest groups, the incentives on their members, the possibility of free-riding on group action, and the greater effectiveness of smaller lobbying groups. See also Olson's 1984 book, *The Rise and Decline of Nations*, which applies his theories to practical political and economic issues.

Riker, William H. (1962), *The Theory of Political Coalitions*. A pathbreaking book which explains why politicians rationally seek to form minimum winning coalitions, and explores the nature of coalitions.

ABOUT THE IEA

The Institute is a research and educational charity (No. CC 235 351), limited by guarantee. Its mission is to improve understanding of the fundamental institutions of a free society by analysing and expounding the role of markets in solving economic and social problems.

The IEA achieves its mission by:

- a high-quality publishing programme
- conferences, seminars, lectures and other events
- outreach to school and college students
- brokering media introductions and appearances

The IEA, which was established in 1955 by the late Sir Antony Fisher, is an educational charity, not a political organisation. It is independent of any political party or group and does not carry on activities intended to affect support for any political party or candidate in any election or referendum, or at any other time. It is financed by sales of publications, conference fees and voluntary donations.

In addition to its main series of publications the IEA also publishes a termly journal, *Economic Affairs*.

The IEA is aided in its work by a distinguished international Academic Advisory Council and an eminent panel of Honorary Fellows. Together with other academics, they review prospective IEA publications, their comments being passed on anonymously to authors. All IEA papers are therefore subject to the same rigorous independent refereeing process as used by leading academic journals.

IEA publications enjoy widespread classroom use and course adoptions in schools and universities. They are also sold throughout the world and often translated/reprinted.

Since 1974 the IEA has helped to create a worldwide network of 100 similar institutions in over 70 countries. They are all independent but share the IEA's mission.

Views expressed in the IEA's publications are those of the authors, not those of the Institute (which has no corporate view), its Managing Trustees, Academic Advisory Council members or senior staff.

Members of the Institute's Academic Advisory Council, Honorary Fellows, Trustees and Staff are listed on the following page.

The Institute gratefully acknowledges financial support for its publications programme and other work from a generous benefaction by the late Alec and Beryl Warren.

Other papers recently published by the IEA include:

The Legal Foundations of Free Markets
Edited by Stephen F. Copp
Hobart Paperback 36; ISBN 978 0 255 36591 8; £15.00

Climate Change Policy: Challenging the Activists
Edited by Colin Robinson
Readings 62; ISBN 978 0 255 36595 6; £10.00

Should We Mind the Gap?
Gender Pay Differentials and Public Policy
J. R. Shackleton
Hobart Paper 164; ISBN 978 0 255 36604 5; £10.00

Pension Provision: Government Failure Around the World
Edited by Philip Booth et al.
Readings 63; ISBN 978 0 255 36602 1; £15.00

New Europe's Old Regions
Piotr Zientara
Hobart Paper 165; ISBN 978 0 255 36617 5; £12.50

Central Banking in a Free Society
Tim Congdon
Hobart Paper 166; ISBN 978 0 255 36623 6; £12.50

Verdict on the Crash: Causes and Policy Implications
Edited by Philip Booth
Hobart Paperback 37; ISBN 978 0 255 36635 9; £12.50

The European Institutions as an Interest Group
The Dynamics of Ever-Closer Union
Roland Vaubel
Hobart Paper 167; ISBN 978 0 255 36634 2; £10.00

An Adult Approach to Education
Alison Wolf
Hobart Paper 168; ISBN 978 0 255 36586 4; £10.00

Taxation and Red Tape
The Cost to British Business of Complying with the UK Tax System
Francis Chittenden, Hilary Foster & Brian Sloan
Research Monograph 64; ISBN 978 0 255 36612 0; £12.50

Ludwig von Mises – A Primer
Eamonn Butler
Occasional Paper 143; ISBN 978 0 255 36629 8; £7.50

Does Britain Need a Financial Regulator?
Statutory Regulation, Private Regulation and Financial Markets
Terry Arthur & Philip Booth
Hobart Paper 169; ISBN 978 0 255 36593 2; £12.50

Hayek's *The Constitution of Liberty*
An Account of Its Argument
Eugene F. Miller
Occasional Paper 144; ISBN 978 0 255 36637 3; £12.50

Fair Trade Without the Froth
A Dispassionate Economic Analysis of 'Fair Trade'
Sushil Mohan
Hobart Paper 170; ISBN 978 0 255 36645 8; £10.00

A New Understanding of Poverty
Poverty Measurement and Policy Implications
Kristian Niemietz
Research Monograph 65; ISBN 978 0 255 36638 0; £12.50

The Challenge of Immigration
A Radical Solution
Gary S. Becker
Occasional Paper 145; ISBN 978 0 255 36613 7; £7.50

Sharper Axes, Lower Taxes
Big Steps to a Smaller State
Edited by Philip Booth
Hobart Paperback 38; ISBN 978 0 255 36648 9; £12.50

Self-employment, Small Firms and Enterprise
Peter Urwin
Research Monograph 66; ISBN 978 0 255 36610 6; £12.50

Crises of Governments
The Ongoing Global Financial Crisis and Recession
Robert Barro
Occasional Paper 146; ISBN 978 0 255 36657 1; £7.50

... and the Pursuit of Happiness
Wellbeing and the Role of Government
Edited by Philip Booth
Readings 64; ISBN 978 0 255 36656 4; £12.50

Other IEA publications

Comprehensive information on other publications and the wider work
of the IEA can be found at www.iea.org.uk. To order any publication
please see below.

Personal customers

Orders from personal customers should be directed to the IEA:
Clare Rusbridge
IEA
2 Lord North Street
FREEPOST LON10168
London SW1P 3YZ
Tel: 020 7799 8907. Fax: 020 7799 2137
Email: crusbridge@iea.org.uk

Trade customers

All orders from the book trade should be directed to the IEA's
distributor:
Gazelle Book Services Ltd (IEA Orders)
FREEPOST RLYS-EAHU-YSCZ
White Cross Mills
Hightown
Lancaster LA1 4XS
Tel: 01524 68765. Fax: 01524 53232
Email: sales@gazellebooks.co.uk

IEA subscriptions

The IEA also offers a subscription service to its publications. For a single
annual payment (currently £42.00 in the UK), subscribers receive every
monograph the IEA publishes. For more information please contact:
Clare Rusbridge
Subscriptions
IEA
2 Lord North Street
FREEPOST LON10168
London SW1P 3YZ
Tel: 020 7799 8907. Fax: 020 7799 2137
Email: crusbridge@iea.org.uk